Prologue

When does a person realise that they are living with a narcissist? When does it change from believing someone loves you and only wants the best for you, to discovering they are a manipulative and controlling bully?

There is a wealth of information about narcissism online. Lists of how to spot one, quizzes to see if you are married to one, and common traits of the behaviour to identify. You can read this information in two ways. Is my husband/boyfriend/family member/friend a narcissist or are they just a complete arsehole?

It can be a fine line for sure, but I believe from my story and the real examples I am going to share, that I can confidently call my ex-husband a Narcissist. Perhaps your conclusion will be different.

I wanted to tell my story to many people out there who are going through the same thing. I originally wanted to write it for myself only, as a form of therapy to assist the healing process, but then realised it may help someone else like me, who may then see there is a way out, as terrifying as it may seem at the time.

Leaving a narcissist is an extremely difficult emotional journey to undertake, and the only way I survived with my sanity intact, is to fully understand everything that would follow on from what I will refer to in the book as Day One. Day One of the Battle. Day One of my life back. Day One of my freedom. Armed with this information was the only way forward.

All the messages quoted in my story are real life, word for word examples taken from messages on my phone, or emails. There is no exaggeration or elaboration, to be honest, I didn't need to do so.

If you are living with someone who controls you, coerces you, disrespects you, then this is the book for you. I hope it will give you the courage to take the steps that I did, to be able to be free yourself from these restraints and begin to take control of your life again, before it's too late. You deserve better.

Chapter One

What is a Narcissist?

So many people have asked me to explain this to them. It is a word I didn't even hear myself until a few years ago and I certainly hadn't known the meaning. Thus, I found it hard to summarise it my own words as it covers such a complex number of behavioural tendencies and traits, and I would end up going off on tangent which would lead to them feeling more confused than ever. In the end I resorted to finding a good summary online, which I shared with them:

'Narcissistic personality disorder is a mental health condition in which people have an unreasonably high sense of their own importance. They need and seek too much attention and want people to admire them. People with this disorder may lack the ability to understand or care about the feelings of others. But behind this mask of extreme confidence, they are not sure of their self-worth and are easily upset by the slightest criticism.

A narcissistic personality disorder causes problems in many areas of life, such as relationships, work, school or financial matters. People with narcissistic personality disorder may be generally unhappy and disappointed when they're not given the special favours or admiration that they believe they deserve. They may find their relationships troubled and unfulfilling, and other people may not enjoy being around them.

Narcissistic personality disorder affects more males than females, and it often begins in the teens or early adulthood. Some children may show traits of narcissism, but this is often typical for their age and doesn't mean they'll go on to develop narcissistic personality disorder.

Symptoms of narcissistic personality disorder and how severe they are can vary. People with the disorder can:

- Have an unreasonably high sense of self-importance and require constant, excessive admiration.
- Feel that they deserve privileges and special treatment.
- Expect to be recognized as superior even without achievements.
- Make achievements and talents seem bigger than they are.
- Be preoccupied with fantasies about success, power, brilliance, beauty or the perfect mate.
- Believe they are superior to others and can only spend time with or be understood by equally special people.
- Be critical of and look down on people they feel are not important.
- Expect special favours and expect other people to do what they want without questioning them.
- Take advantage of others to get what they want.
- Have an inability or unwillingness to recognise the needs and feelings of others.

- Be envious of others and believe others envy them.
- Behave in an arrogant way, brag a lot and come across as conceited.
- Insist on having the best of everything — for instance, the best car or office.

At the same time, people with narcissistic personality disorder have trouble handling anything they view as criticism. They can:

- Become impatient or angry when they don't receive special recognition or treatment.
- Have major problems interacting with others and easily feel slighted.
- React with rage or contempt and try to belittle other people to make themselves appear superior.
- Have difficulty managing their emotions and behaviour.
- Experience major problems dealing with stress and adapting to change.

- Withdraw from or avoid situations in which they might fail.
- Feel depressed and moody because they fall short of perfection.
- Have secret feelings of insecurity, shame, humiliation, and fear of being exposed as a failure. (1)

Now they got it.

People have asked me questions recently such as: 'How did you not see the signs? Weren't there any red flags?'

It doesn't really work like that. I generally believed that every relationship starting out has an element of insecurity, of risk. But I was the type of person who followed my gut instinct, my heart usually winning over my head. I craved happiness and made everything fit because I wanted it to. A mistake I will never make again.

Chapter Two

In the beginning

Up to 2009, I likened my relationship history to a CV.

It was relatively straightforward. It was neat, concise, and I spent a reasonable time with each one with no dramatic reasons for leaving. I had never been sacked, and I had left each job in an amicable way, with no hard feelings.

Then 2009 rolled around. I started dating a guy who I had known nearly all my life through our school years, and from living only a few doors away when growing up. The relationship developed quickly, and we moved in together after only seeing each other for a few months, but very quickly, cracks started to appear. He would constantly have other girls messaging and calling him. He would always lay his phone face down when he was near me. Something always just felt 'off.'

I had never been jealous in a relationship before, but I couldn't get rid of this niggling feeling that ate away at me, day by day. I started to ask him who was messaging him often, and as a result he became more and more secretive about his whereabouts. I never felt like he was ever being completely honest with me.

He was the most laid-back, easy-going person I knew, but he was a bad drunk, almost like an alter ego. He would be cocky, arrogant, scathing. Nothing at all like his sober self. He never took me out with his friends when they went out as couples. It was nearly always just the two of us. I found that odd. It was like he was hiding me away and I couldn't understand why. I pushed these things to the back of my mind as much as I could, as apart from that we had a good life, travelled frequently, and had a lot in common.

About a year into the relationship, my mum was diagnosed with advanced stage 4 cancer. We were shell shocked. She had experienced some issues with her legs in the bones and we thought she had osteoporosis. After many scans we found out it was bone cancer. What we didn't know at first is that you can't just *get* bone cancer. It must be a secondary cancer which meant it came from elsewhere. Later we found out it was breast cancer, which had been undetected even following a recent mammogram.

My life was turned upside down. Friends and family rallied around my parents and me, but nothing shook the deep fear inside of me that never went away. I needed emotional support from my boyfriend, but he seemed unable to give it to me. My doubts about the relationship festered. I became withdrawn, and my job was suffering. I started smoking again despite having stopped 5 years earlier. We became more and more distant as the cancer journey became more and more of a rollercoaster journey within my family. We lived our lives between appointments, hoping for positive news. Sometimes we had a ray of light – maybe the cancer had got smaller – we would celebrate until the next appointment, which wouldn't always be so cheery.

In hindsight, I probably wasn't much fun to live with at the time. I couldn't be happy, or plan anything in the future. My mum was living on borrowed time and that was that. In 2011 we planned a trip away to London to see the new years eve fireworks, something I had always wanted to do. We booked into a famous Michelin star Indian restaurant; it was the perfect weekend. Or it should have been. We went to the wrong part of London for midnight. We heard the fireworks; we just didn't see them.

The next night when we went to the restaurant, he told me out of the blue that it was over and there was no going back. Shocked was an understatement. Apart from the hideous timing, I had no idea he was unhappy. He told me I was no longer fun to be around. Looking back, I realise just how self-absorbed and selfish that sounded given what was happening in my life, but that was that. It was how he felt, and he had clearly already made up his mind. We got the train home the next morning. I was numb. Happy New Year.

He agreed to let me keep my stuff at his house until I found somewhere to live, while I slept in my parent's spare room, with our dog. It was one of the lowest points of my life. I would wake up every morning thinking it was all a bad dream, until I felt the cold nose of my puppy on my face, awaking me to the sight of my parents' magnolia walls of the spare room, which in other times had been a happy space.

Within days of being apart, he was already going out, buying new clothes, and as I later found out, going on dates. He had obviously checked out of this relationship a lot earlier than I realised.

I moped around for the first few months. He was a property landlord, so he found me a house himself and organised everything for me. It was little comfort, but it gave me hope that we may get back together. When it became glaringly obvious this wasn't happening, I gradually started to pull myself together and think about the future. I decided at that point a few months later to join a dating app. A terrifying thought, but what was the worst that could happen?

Chapter Three

Plenty of Fish

I met him on April 9th, 2012. It was Easter Monday. It was only a single day after I had joined the dating app and he was the first person I spoke to. He looked nice on his profile. We agreed to meet for a drink. For the first time in several months, I felt excited about the prospect of meeting someone new.

We met locally, as we happened to live in the same village. I remember my surprise at how he greeted me when I entered the pub. Dismissive, almost. No real greeting, no kiss on the cheek and little eye contact. He seemed to be very friendly with the bar staff so I knew he must come here a lot. I shrugged it off assuming nerves rather than arrogance.

As the evening went on, it seemed like we had a lot in common. He was going through a divorce and told me he had only just really started online dating again but hadn't taken the plunge, as such. He came across as a genuine guy, trying to build his life back up following his previous marriage from which he also had two children. He told me his wife had been unfaithful. Bitch. It sounded like he had been through a lot, and I genuinely sympathised with his story, which he told with such conviction. We talked a lot about music. Both interrupting each other as we suddenly had so much to say. A man approached us on his way out and slipped us a note. It said that he could tell we were a happy couple who clearly understood each other and was positive about our happy future. Bit weird, but nice.

The night flew by. He asked me if I wanted to watch a film with him at his house, *The Da Vinci Code*, to be precise. but I declined. It was too soon. He did however offer me a spare microwave as he had ended up with two following his divorce, and I was without. I accepted this offer, much to his amusement. We drove to collect it and said goodnight. I felt positive about where it may lead, and if we would see each other again.

He called me the next morning on his way to work. Light-hearted, chatty. We arranged a second date, which went well. Before we knew it, we were seeing each other regularly and I was introduced quickly to the children, and some of his closest friends. Things felt good.

The first time I ever remember him behaving in a controlling way, was about 3 weeks after we had met. I had planned to go on a night out with friends and was at home getting ready. He called me; his kids were in the car, and I was on speakerphone. He told me he was on his way to my house, and we were all going out for dinner. I don't know why, but I didn't tell him I was busy. Maybe I thought it was romantic, or flattered he was being so spontaneous and wanted to see me. At the chagrin of my friends, I told them I was working late and got ready for his imminent arrival.

About 6 weeks into the relationship, we were asleep at his house when we heard loud, persistent banging on the front door. I jumped up and looked outside, to see a girl standing in the road, looking up at the bedroom window. I asked him who the hell it was, and he admitted he had had a fling with a local girl but it was well and truly over and she had now taking to stalking him. She knocked and knocked and eventually left. Thoughts flooded into my mind as to why she hadn't been mentioned before. I fleetingly wondered if she was the only one, and for the first time I felt uneasy about our new relationship. It niggled me for some time, but eventually I just told myself I was being paranoid, and I had no reason not to give him the benefit of the doubt. It clearly hadn't been serious enough to feel like it was relevant to us, and he seemed laid back about her late-night visit.

He told me early on in the relationship that he was searching for the perfect woman. He was certain she existed. She would be 5 foot tall, no more. I am 5 foot 4. He made it clear that I was not that woman, but I would probably do for now. For some reason I laughed it off, surely these random things that he came out with weren't really how he felt, were they? It must just be some sort of arrogance or banter, I thought.

He had been in the Army for 13 years. I respected him for it, proud of what he achieved and what he had experienced. I listened to his many stories, looked at his photographs.

In years to come I would realise that his experience was a likely contributor for his behaviour to come. He believed that being ex-military was far superior to us civilians, or 'civvies' - a word I eventually came to despise. He would use it always in a derogatory way, like civilians were stupid, uneducated, naïve. Much later in our relationship I noticed that he treated his army friends differently to us civvies. If his army mates came to stay with us, he would be the perfect host. He would pull out all the stops, entertain, cook breakfast even. For the civvies, it was left to me to host, and often he wouldn't even be in the same room.

On one occasion a civvie couple were staying with us and he was still in bed on the Sunday morning when we all had breakfast. Hungover, as usual. He woke to see we had used up all the eggs. For army friends he probably would have dismissed it but on this occasion, this particular friend was ordered to go to the shop and buy more.

Things were going great. We had been on holiday, on many nights out including with the children, when 5 months in, he dumped me by text. No real explanation, just that things didn't feel right. I was taken aback, I thought things were going really well and I was more upset than I expected to be.

We still continued to message each other on and off and one night he turned up at my house after he had been to the pub. He stayed the night. We decided to be friends, business partners. We had grown a business idea to be property landlords together and had started the process on a small scale. I accepted this and was happy that he remained in my life to some extent.

After 6 months together, I got the shock of my life. I was pregnant. It was my first day at a new job. We barely knew each other really and I was terrified. I was working away when I took a test and it couldn't wait I until I got home, I had to tell him and get it over with. It was probably the scariest phone call I have had to make in my life so far. I knew he wouldn't be pleased either.

We met a few days later in the pub to talk. He told me he didn't want any more kids. He also told me that he didn't really fancy me deep down and that I was more of a best mate than anything, but he felt that he needed me to be in his life. I found this confusing. We had a good sex life, and it didn't add up in my head. Most people would have left at that point and moved on. Why would anyone be with someone who isn't even attracted to them? But I didn't.

At first, I considered not going ahead with the pregnancy. He came with me to a clinic to discuss the options available. While we were in the waiting room, he fell asleep. Charming. His phone started ringing, and it was the girl who had turned up at the house that night. What on earth was going on here? He shrugged it off, pleading ignorance.

After careful consideration, I decided I wanted to keep the baby. I was 34 and had the biological clock ringing in my ears. Maybe it was now or never? What if this was my only chance? He confirmed that if that was the case, he didn't want anything to do with any of it. I was ok with that and started to get my head around living alone with a baby and began looking for a new house. One night, he came home from work and told me he had changed his mind. He said he wanted me to move in with him and see how things went and take it from there. I agreed, thinking it was the right thing to do. We told his kids. His daughter was 12 at the time and exited at the prospect of a baby brother or sister. His son, who was 9, was indifferent which we expected.

I remember when he told his friends about the pregnancy. I expected congratulations, but instead all I got was pity, and looks of sympathy.

He wasn't the easiest person to live with. He was critical about everything, yet lazy himself. He was a complete paradox when it came to things like housework. I knew he was capable of looking after himself, of cooking and cleaning, but suddenly it was my job.

He would complain that I hadn't hoovered properly and would deliberately leave a piece of rubbish on the floor to see how many days it would stay there, rather than dealing with it himself, or helping. He would fly into a rage if he couldn't find something in the house, emptying drawers all over the floor, throwing things and expecting me to clear up the mess. Breaking things that didn't work for him, smashing them up in temper.

The pregnancy itself was free of drama, but he started to use me as a convenience. I became the designated driver every weekend, sometimes being called out at 1am to pick him up steaming from the pub. He was made redundant when I was about 4 months pregnant, and sat around the house, sulking and sometimes barely conversing with me for days, between working at my full-time job. There were days I would cry in the bedroom, wondering if I had made a terrible mistake.

It took some time for him to find a new job. He was what I called a 'square peg in a round hole' when it came to employment. It is a common scenario for those who have been in the army to fit in easily in 'normal' society.

He was no exception. When we met, he worked for a teaching company – the ones who made him redundant - delivering qualifications to adults. Before that, he worked at the local college and left due to not getting on with the female staff, in particular, his superior. Before that, he was in the Police, and so was his wife.

The exit from this job was by far the most serious. One day whilst on a late shift, him and a colleague ran a red light to get home faster; it was late, and the roads were empty. They were clocked going through it, which they knew could lead to disciplinary action. To get out of it, he called in a fake job which would excuse them from the light and allow them to pass through it legitimately. Job done. Or not, it would seem. His colleague couldn't live with the lie and reported it. He was in trouble. He went to court and received a suspended sentence and community service. He said the court made an example of him. He was forced to resign, criminal record in hand. He always blamed the colleague for reporting him, never himself for committing the offence.

One day, while I was at work, I received a cryptic message from one of my oldest friends. She said there was something she needed to tell me. I was intrigued and slightly nervous. I couldn't even imagine what it may be, she sounded solemn. She called me. She asked me to cast my mind back to 2008. Her little sister was preparing to get married to the love of her life. They had been together for years and were finally tying the knot. She reminded me of an incident a month or so before the wedding which had caused huge upset. The sister had recently started a new job at the police station, on the reception. Suddenly, she was on her phone a lot, which her fiancé noticed. Something made him go through the itemised phone bill from her number - back in the day when that's what we did - where he noticed one number coming up. Over and over, hundreds and hundreds of messages.

Yes, I said, how could I forget? The wedding was nearly called off completely. She was devastated, protested her innocence, it was nothing, she insisted. We had read between the lines, figured someone had showed her some attention and she had naively gone along with it. She certainly wasn't the cheating type. Eventually little sister was forgiven, and the wedding went ahead as planned. For the record they are still happily married. I wondered why my friend was telling me this. The man in question was married, his wife was also in the Police. Oh.

It was him. My boyfriend. Father of my unborn child. He was the texter. How the hell had I not known this? Why had nobody told me when I met him? I never found out why really, but it didn't really matter now. I knew he had met the little sister before, we had a few friends in common. He never said anything other than she was a nice girl, he like her. End of story. Wow.

I asked him about it. He laughed it off, said they were friends and that nothing had ever happened. He didn't seem to think that the fact he nearly had their wedding called off was an issue. It took me a long time to process this. I had known this girl since I was 6 years old, and I believed her. I messaged her and we cleared the air, I had no issue with her, but I was on guard if we ever bumped into her, I doubted that awkward feeling would ever leave.

When I was 5 months pregnant, my mum died. She had managed to live for 4 terrifying years through her battle with cancer. I was devastated. I had desperately hoped she would have lived long enough to be here when my baby was born. For years she had dreamed I would have children. My brother had several, but it wasn't the same, she would explain. I took comfort in the fact that she at least knew we were having a boy, and she knew what his name would be. I needed emotional support now more than ever. He was great. He finally started to take care of me in the way I needed. He helped out with the funeral arrangements and gave me the emotional support I needed and encouraged me to stay positive through the remaining months of the pregnancy.

For the first couple of weeks after my son was born, he was the perfect dad, cooking and looking after the house, food shopping and doing what he needed. He had just started a new job and his mood was much improved. One thing he wouldn't do however, was wake up with the baby in the night. My son didn't sleep through the night for three exhausting years and not once did he get up in the night to feed or soothe him. Not once. If I ever asked him why or if he could help, his response was always the same 'You should have swallowed.' Nice.

He believed that because he didn't 'ask' for this child in his life, it was my responsibility and mine to deal with forever. It was so selfish. I remember being shocked at how self-involved he could be. A few weeks into the new job, he brought home a work mate during their lunch hour. The baby was only a few weeks old, and given my nightly routine, I was permanently exhausted. I was surviving on coffee until he threw my machine in the bin for not cleaning it.

He started cooking in the kitchen. It was only beans on toast, but I was ravenous and hadn't had the time or energy to cook anything for myself yet. I joined his workmate at the dining table, eagerly awaiting my lunch. He put down the plates on the table, one for him, one for the workmate. I looked at him. Where's mine? I asked. He laughed, saying that they were working, I had all day to sort myself out. I was furious. How could he have done that? Maybe my hormones and emotions were getting the better of me, but I knew that I would have never done that to him. I just wasn't a factor; I was just the one holding the baby.

Birthdays and other occasions were a strange thing in this new family. He gave me the impression that when he was growing up, they weren't celebrated, or they weren't happy events. I was always the opposite and loved an excuse to celebrate, and spoil everyone. On my birthday I was lucky if I got a gift in the first few years, and certainly never a card. If we went out for a meal or drink it would be me who would organise it, or it wouldn't happen. One year, he completely forgot my birthday. He only found out when his boss told him than evening, after she had seen it on Facebook. It just showed me how self-involved he was. One year, much more recently, I got the shock of my life when he threw me a surprise party. There were friends, and those in the UK sent video messages. I loved it all. He loved the credit, of course, what a good husband he was, what a great party!

Mother's Day was my main source of heartache. Since losing my mum, it felt empty. I tried to console myself that I would at least be a mother myself for the next one and would get to enjoy it in a way I never had. Not the case. I stupidly hoped for a token gift or a card from my son. He was clearly two young to think for himself and hoped his dad would do that, as so many others did.

Every year I would avoid Facebook because I couldn't bear to see the endless Mother's Day posts, the appreciation posts, the love these families projected on to their mum on this day. I felt invisible, unloved, unworthy of anyone celebrating my role as a mother. Maybe I wasn't good enough at it? I didn't know. He never told me I was doing a good job or gave me encouragement and support on difficult days. I just 'cracked on' and did what I needed to do.'

Chapter Four

Jealous Guy

The first time I saw his jealous side come through was from regular socialising at his sports club. There was a guy there who thought he was god's gift. He worked for the same company as me and had put in a good word for me to secure an interview. He was popular with women, and overconfident. We would chat at a group level, nearly always with my boyfriend present. Easy, everyday subjects, apart from one occasion where he was telling us about his latest conquests, in far too much detail. I didn't want to hear it, but we were told anyway. That night, we went home, and I had no idea what was to come. He verbally laid into me, accusing me of flirting. I was shocked and taken aback, I couldn't think of a single point in the evening where that may have come across like that. I stood my ground; told him he was being paranoid. We argued and he left the house, and spent the rest of the night at the pub. I assume so anyway, looking back he could have gone anywhere for all I know.

Little did I know that this was only the beginning. The jealousy grew and grew within him, the longer we were together. He would start commenting if I was on my phone, wondering who I was messaging. I didn't like it. I don't have a jealous bone in my body and was confused at why his thoughts were leading him that way. I was always led to believe that those who show jealousy are often the ones who are up to something, which makes them believe the other person probably is, too. I fleetingly wondered about the two girls who had cast doubts in my mind previously but dismissed them quickly. Ignorance is bliss, I told myself.

We spent all our free time together, either as a family or as a couple. I rarely went out with friends anymore, only if we doubled up with another couple, that's just how it was. He had no reason to ever think I was even close to anyone else. He wouldn't stay at home and look after our son if I wanted to go out without him, that's for sure.

He would constantly refer back to his ex-wife. Because she had been unfaithful, he didn't trust that I wouldn't do the same. Every scenario was a comparison to her. I would ask him not to compare me, explaining that we were two different women, and this was two different relationships. I understood where the mistrust came from, given my suspicions of my ex, but I was able to separate the two, and trust him until proven otherwise. He struggled to do the same for me. I had to earn my trust, which I should have realised, was a task that would never ever come to end.

I had even received a text message from a woman when I was pregnant. She was the ex-wife of his ex-brother-in-law. She told me to be careful and that he was a womaniser. When I asked him about her, he told me she fancied him and had previously put it on a plate for him and he refused. I believed him, I had no reason not to.

A few months after my son was born, he left his Facebook account open on my laptop and curiosity got the better of me. There were suggestive messages to a married woman who I knew he used to live near and that he told me he fancied in the past. I confronted him about it, and he brushed it off. That niggling feeling was back again. I wondered if it was simply projection, but I didn't want to overthink it.

For a few years I had made some money doing a second job as a wedding photographer. My portfolio and reputation had built up quickly and it was starting to be something I really loved. It meant working many Saturdays which I knew wouldn't be a problem as when we had first met, he told me that Saturdays were his sport days and not to expect anything from him on those days.

For some reason he would always be in a strange mood on the day of a wedding. He would be quiet in the morning, rarely respond to messages or calls while I was doing the job, and moody when I returned home. I had asked him about it before, but he said there was no issue, I was imagining it. Maybe I was.

On one occasion, my assistant had let me down and I asked him if he wanted to come and help me. Nothing technical, just managing the crowd and helping to pull groups together. No problem.

He was little use. He spent almost the entire day chatting up the wedding events organiser because she allegedly had a 'good arse.' I was humiliated at the blatancy of it and frustrated at his lack of assistance. I didn't invite him again.

His moods however got worse as time went on. He would ask if I had been chatted up by any of the guests or offered a drink. Part of my job was to talk to the guests, and I was an outgoing chatty person at the weddings, which was mainly why I was liked by my customers. I would reassure him every time that I remained professional at all times, though in my mind I was wondering why I had to keep justifying myself, especially given his love of flirting and chatting up strangers. It was a perfect example of double standards.

He would always criticize the photographs when they were finished, no matter how delighted the happy couple were. It wasn't that he could do any better, and I did not understand initially what motivated him to pull me down so much about it.

But then I realised. I was better than him at something, something he couldn't compete with. Even years later if I took a picture of something on my phone and it didn't come out perfectly, he would look at it and say, 'call yourself a photographer?'

We could be driving, and we would pass some beautiful scenery. He would tell me to take a picture immediately.

If I wasn't quicker, or the shot was blurred due to being in a moving car, out the phrase would come again. It was like he was constantly telling me that I couldn't do my job.

Chapter Five

Bon Voyage

In 2016, we moved abroad after I was offered a new job. It seemed like a great opportunity to start a new life and my son was only 3 and seemed the perfect age for him to experience it. We had discussed living away for a while and this was too good to pass up. We had tried to emigrate to Australia, but after a year of paperwork, we were declined at the final stage.

The sea air, the humidity and the smell of this new country was heady. I couldn't believe we were here. We had never visited the place before and were keen to explore. It had so much history, so much to discover and this was now our home. We were never scared about leaving to come here, one thing we had in common was that we were not afraid to take risks. It was an adventure for us, and I knew it would be great for us as a family. He didn't ask his other children how they felt, not to my knowledge. We only saw them every two weeks as they still lived their mum, and he felt like he was at the bottom of the list when it came to their priorities. They were teenagers now, living their own lives.

We loved our new home at first; we lived in a small community, and I made friends quickly through my job, as many were British. He was still commuting back to the UK for work, so I was on my own through the week, but I loved the contrast of having my own space for once, but also looked forward to him coming home at the weekend, as we always had a lot to talk about and catch up on.

After around 18 months the job didn't work out and the small community we had loved at first began to feel claustrophobic. People we thought were friends started to show a different side to their personality and we didn't like it. He didn't have any friends of his own, they were all a by-product of my friendships there. We had hoped he would find a job there, but it was notoriously difficult as opportunities were scarce for the work he did.

In 2018 we left the area and moved north to a popular coastal resort closer to a major airport which would benefit his commute. The sea was a dazzling blue, unlike where we started. The air was clean, and fresh and the scenery breath-taking. I felt we had definitely made the right choice moving. We didn't know anyone here, but I knew it wouldn't take me long to find friends. I joined mums' clubs on Facebook and enrolled our son in school which led to many friendships with other parents.

I didn't have a job at first, but he earnt enough for us both for now, so I enjoyed the extra time I had with my son for the first time since he was born. He was now 5. As the months went by, I started to feel bored and lost, I felt like I had no purpose left in life, was this it for me? A mother and girlfriend until I die? He was happy with the way things were, he would come home to a clean house, food on the table, everything sorted out for him. He saw himself as the 'provider.' I took care of everything, our legal paperwork, our residential legalities, the admin associated with rent, bills, and everything else. But it wasn't enough for me, I needed to work too.

I started to focus on my weight and health and saw an opportunity to create an online business which I felt had some decent earnings potential. It was primarily based on social media. He wasn't overly interested at first but saw the benefits once I started making a good wage from it. He had a good job, and a good salary and this balanced things out nicely.

We had a great lifestyle, we were happy. We weren't arguing, our son was making friends and so were we. I used to say to him that life with him was never boring. I meant it. He could be a lot of fun to be around, always had a story or joke to tell. He liked being the centre of attention, not even caring if sometimes the joke was on him.

Over time, that statement was still true. Life was never boring, but 'fun' slowly turned into 'drama.'

Chapter Six

Fancy a drink?

As the years flew by, I realised just how much he drank. In our early months we drank together, it was normal, social. Fun. This seemed to change over time, and I could see that he punctuated everything with a drink. Pissed off? Drink. Made redundant? Drink. New job? Drink. Tuesday 2pm? Drink. Don't get me wrong, I like a drink too. But I drink for enjoyment, and that alone. He used to refer to himself as a 'social hand grenade' One night, the pin came out and became the first of two occasions where I potentially saved his life.

Living abroad, it was so easy to drink and stay out late, even with children. It was completely normal. Locals would be out at bars and restaurants with babies and children into the early hours, it was just how it was.

One night we were at a local bar and restaurant where we went to almost daily. We knew all the staff and felt at home there, and they were great with kids. After a few hours on the beer, he started drinking

Sambuca shots along with the husband of my friend. A switch seemed to flick and suddenly he was incoherent. He lifted and flipped a glass table and chairs on the restaurant terrace. We had to get him out of there. The friend's husband was in a similar state, falling onto a sofa and nearly crushing our son. He was still only 4 years old at the time. I managed to get us all into a taxi and back out to walk the short walk home. My son needed the toilet and I had to get into the apartment quickly. We left him sat on the path outside the flat and I had to leave him there for a minute. I couldn't get him standing up no matter how hard I tried.

I was angry at him and considered leaving him there for longer while I went into the apartment to put my son to bed, but instead we went back downstairs to get him. He had fallen back on the pavement and was laid on his back, choking on his own vomit. A young couple happened to be walking past and quickly called an ambulance and he was taken to the local hospital. As my son and I sat in the room with him, my son asked if daddy was dead. I can only thank my lucky stars that he only now has a vague memory of this.

When he came round, he was furious with me for making him go to hospital. He didn't understand and would not admit what had just happened. He said I was overreacting. I felt helpless, exhausted. I just wanted to go to bed. The next day he took chocolates to the ambulance staff to apologise for his behaviour. No word of apology to me, no chocolates either, for that matter.

A regular habit of his when we had been out in the afternoon after school or early evening, was to continue drinking when we got home. I would put our son to bed, and then sometimes I would join him but when it got late, I had had enough. In the later years he did it more often, into the early hours, sometimes to 5am. The music would be blaring, and our son wouldn't be able to sleep. I would repeatedly ask him to turn it down, but it was pointless. He believed he had the right to do what he wanted in his own home. He didn't care if he kept us awake, it didn't affect him.

Chapter Seven

Marital Bliss

We were married in 2019. Despite everything, and a turbulent six years, I still thought it was what I wanted. I wanted my son to have the same surname as me and for us to be a 'proper' family. That morning, my dad said to me that it wasn't too late to change my mind. I thought he was joking but now wonder if he saw something I didn't. It was however a lovely, intimate wedding, I had organised most of it and had paid for it with my money from my online business. I loved having all our friends and family around us for the first time in a long time, and they flew to us from as far as Australia and Canada.

His groom's speech was a lengthy one, and there were some lovely words in it. Anyone listening would think wow, they sound like they have the perfect relationship. I felt emotional during it because it felt like he was finally seeing me for who I was and what I had done for him in the last 7 years. It felt good and I felt happy. The way he delivered it however was somewhat unconventional. He didn't stand at his place at the top table, as is the tradition. No, he worked the room. It was a bit like watching a motivational speaker, one of those where everyone ends up chanting and clapping at the end. He even stopped mid-speech to have a go at someone who dared to speak for a second during it. Not an army friend, of course.

I barely saw him for most of the day, and as I expected he was the last man standing, wasted. He spent most of it at the bar with the army friends. We were the last to leave and he deliberately smashed his glass on the floor as we left the venue, for no apparent reason. Me and one of his friends had to practically carry him back to the hotel, where he passed out in bed immediately.

The honeymoon was horrendous to say the least. It was like a switch had flicked since we were married. From day one of the trip, he was childlike, throwing tantrums like a toddler. We went away with another couple, a close army friend and his wife who had also recently got married. He was constantly being difficult, not wanting to do anything that we all did, and flying off into a rage for no reason.

On the first night he argued with me because I didn't want to go to a nightclub. He smashed his sunglasses and walked out of the bar, leaving me alone at 1am in the morning. I cried more on that honeymoon than I ever had. I remember sitting there thinking 'what the fuck have I done??'

On the second night, we went to the famous Café Del Mar in Ibiza to watch the sunset. We were there really early, and we were starting to get hungry. I asked him if he wanted to eat but as usual, he didn't – when he drank, he didn't eat. I said I was going to go to a nearby restaurant and grab something with the other couple and we wouldn't be long. When we returned - it couldn't have been any more than hour - he wasn't speaking to me. He accused me of leaving him on his own and that he looked like an idiot. Our friends were taken aback by his behaviour, though he was perfectly nice to them. I ignored it and eventually he came around and was ok for the rest of the evening.

It felt like now I was his wife, he could do what he wanted, behave how he wanted. He kept saying to anyone who would listen that his dad always told him once you're married, the sex stops and it's all downhill from there. Then another phrase about a dressing gown, I fail to remember the exact wording of that one which is surprising, given how often he said it. I always wrote things off to an arrogance or misinterpretation but looking back it was more than that. He genuinely believed he was the most important thing in the world and that he deserved the best of everything. He almost acted like he was hard done by, by now being saddled with a wife. It was confusing, humiliating and upsetting.

On the last day of the trip, he was in the hotel swimming pool while I was sunbathing. He had run out of beer and told me to go to the bar, as he often would. No please or thank you, usually just 'oi!'

I told him he would have to wait. He started throwing water from the pool in my direction, like a petulant child. The wife of the other couple challenged his behaviour and told him he was out of order, and he should show me some respect for once. She told him she was disgusted with the way he spoke to me. They had a blazing argument and they both left the pool area separately in a huff, and I was left alone. Again. I ended up searching the bars in the town and eventually found him, already worse for wear. After the honeymoon he was apologetic and admitted it didn't go well and that he would make it up to me one day. I accepted the apology; it was rare for him to admit his behaviour, so I moved on.

I found that in general I would make excuses for his behaviour to those close to me. I would laugh off his derogatory comments, his demanding ways. He drank Guinness and would always cause a drama in any bar where it wasn't acceptable or poured correctly and send it back. I'm sure bar staff used to groan when he walked into the pub. But we laughed it off, it was just one of his 'ways'.

A year or so later, one night stands out to me when we were still living abroad. It was a Sunday afternoon and the three of us had been out together and as usual he had drunk too much in the afternoon. We had plans to go to a local quiz that we went to regularly. He was being annoying, loud, winding me up deliberately but I was ignoring him, not letting him get the reaction he so wanted. Nobody around us gave him that attention he craved, either. He always used to buy people drinks, spending hundreds some nights, it was like he wanted everyone to know he could afford it, that he was important, and thought it would make him popular and respected. It did neither. They didn't want the drinks and they never bought them back, not many, anyway.

Eventually he got a taxi home without even telling me he was leaving. I stayed on with my son to do the quiz and we had a great night. We left at 8.15pm and I messaged him to say I was walking home. 10 minutes later we arrived home and I got into bed with him, but he was snoring loudly, so I went into the spare room, which happened often. My son heard me and got into bed with me. About 2 hours later I heard my phone beeping with several text messages:

22.50pm: 'Still walking home? Don't come near my bed. Night! 2112....Walking home now. 2352.....No home home. Please do NOT come near me'

Drunken rambling, it made no sense. I was upstairs in bed. My phone beeped again:

22.58pm: 'Liar'
22.58pm: 'Liar'
22.58pm: 'Liar'
22.58pm: 'Liar'
22.59pm: 'Fuck you'.
22.59pm: 'Say hi to Steve.'

Steve? Steve was a mutual friend who we had known for a few years. They played golf together. I had barely spoke to him that night.

I walked downstairs and he was there in the kitchen, putting his shoes on. I asked what the hell he was playing at. He told me he thought I was still in the bar, with my son. His eyes were wild, still drunken but filled with rage and purpose. We argued and I went back to bed. Around 10 minutes later I woke to find him standing over the bed watching us, his breathing heavy. I pretended to be asleep. For the first time I feared what he may do, I didn't recognise him. For years he had told my son and I that he was here to protect us, to take care of us. Ironic that I now felt more afraid of him than anyone in the world.

Chapter Eight

2020 - Lockdown

In most of our years together we had rarely lived together full time. He had started another job just after our son was born, which meant he worked away in the week, and had always commuted when we left the UK. I often wonder if our relationship survived so long because of this, that I had never really seen his true colours from only seeing him at weekends. The pandemic however, meant he would stay with us, all in one country, all together. Having him at home was a novelty at first, but it soon wore off. He drank more than ever, sleeping until after lunch. Every meal I cooked was open to criticism, yet he never bothered doing any cooking himself.

He would sneak out to meet some of the lads from the local, to drink and get out, despite the strict rules imposed on us. One day he took our son with him. They were out for several hours and he came back absolutely smashed. I wasn't impressed.

A year after we were married, my best friend managed to fly over and stay with us when some of the lockdown restrictions were lifted. I hadn't seen her since the wedding, and I was excited to catch up. We had just moved house and had our own pool; the weather was just getting to the perfect temperature, and I couldn't wait to have her around.

On the second night she was there, he went to bed and me and her stayed up chatting and talking about old times. As girls do, we were laughing about old boyfriends, looking on Facebook and groaning about bad exes. At some point, He had quietly opened the bedroom door and was eavesdropping. Later when I went to bed, I could tell there was something wrong. He muttered something about us talking and in my heart, I just knew he had been listening. I didn't care, we had only been reminiscing and I had nothing to worry about what I had talked about.

The next day was horrendous. He had only heard snippets of conversation and had woven these snippets into a completely different story. He accused me of still messaging ex boyfriends and I told him he had completely misheard. He left the house early, and I had no idea where he had gone. As usual, my day was then filled with vicious text messages about what he claimed he had heard. I went to the beach with my friend and tried to ignore it, but I was in a foul mood for the rest of the day.

When we got home later, he had been back home and gone out again. My friend opened the kitchen cupboard to find all my underwear in the bin. I messaged him and asked what the hell he was doing and as always was accused of not having sex with him enough so what was the point in having nice underwear? My friend called her boyfriend who was staying in a different part of Spain and asked him to collect her. She couldn't bear to be around this atmosphere, and I didn't blame her at all. He had ruined her trip already. I had things planned for her and I, and I just wanted to cry. He couldn't stand the fact that my attention was on her and not him. He was jealous.

We argued at length. He even said that he was planning on messaging the woman in the UK whose messages I had read years before. I wanted to scream in frustration.

Eventually, he accepted that he had misheard, though I don't think he really thought that; he would never ever doubt his views, but he let it drop. In conversation later that day, he mentioned when he had been out all day when he was ignoring me, he had lunch with a girl he had bumped into who we barely knew. All the while as I was in turmoil, and upset at the way he was acting, he was wining and dining someone else.

Now that lockdown was finally lifting, I started going on long morning walks with one of my closest friends. It felt amazing to be outside, and we used these mornings to explore the town, the hills and countryside. He would be working those mornings, and he hated it. If I was more than an hour I would get a text, or call asking where we were, why were we out for such a long time? When would I be back? One day on our walk we had found a beautiful spot high above the town and wanted to take a photo of us with the scenery behind us. We set up my phone to use the timer, perching it on a rock and frantically running back to the frame before the lens clicked. We laughed as it took several attempts to get the right shot, but we did, eventually.

When I showed him the photo later that day, he was convinced someone had taken the picture, how could we have taken it ourselves? I explained about the timer, but I could tell he wasn't convinced. He was on permanent suspicious mode at all times.

Chapter Nine

Self esteem

I never felt confident or good about myself when I was with him. Apart from the fact that I was 4 inches too tall for his 'perfect woman' profile, he would tell me I was overweight, or tell me what I was wearing didn't look good on me. He told me I had a fat arse and that my boobs were saggy, for years he encouraged me to get plastic surgery. He wanted me to wear high heels every single day, regardless. The only time he would suggest outfits for me was from sexy underwear sites. He would order lingerie which was two sizes too small for me then have a go at me for not wearing it for him.

When I first met him, he hated any form of physical attention. He wouldn't hold my hand or put a hand on my leg if we were on the sofa. We rarely kissed. I felt he was just guarded, and not wanting to let himself become too emotionally involved. Years later this changed, but by this point I was almost conditioned to not do it, to not want it. Near the end of our relationship if he showed me affection, it made my skin crawl. It was too little, too late.

Something which I became numb to, but I know would upset others around us, was his attitude towards other women when I was around. If an attractive girl appeared, he would say 'smash' (an army term I believe). This could happen up to 20 times a day. For years I asked him to stop but he refused. He would do it even if it was just me and him. Or in front of our son. It was like a game, making me feel inadequate or trying to get a reaction. He would tell me that someone had a good arse, or tits and what did I think? I would pretend that his constant comments about women didn't bother me. Of course, it did, I was only human after all.

I was slowly becoming a doormat; a pushover and I didn't even realise it. I had always been a strong-willed, independent person, feisty when I needed to be, but I had a very laid-back side to my personality which was exploited to the hilt. They say that narcissists tend to be attracted to strong, independent, successful people. It's almost a challenge to reduce that person to a meek, pathetic shadow of their former self. I feel like that was exactly what happened to me.

'They like to have relationships with stronger people because when they are able to tear them down, they feel even stronger and more powerful than if the person was someone who is weak. You have to remember that narcissists are all about their image, and they will go to any lengths to ensure that image is a good one. Toward that end, they will zero in on particular strengths they see in other people and then proceed to destroy the very strengths they admire. People with strong family relationships, good careers, and a strong sense of accomplishment all attract the narcissist's attention' (2)

There would be no way I could ever comment that another man was attractive. He would ask if I thought men were attractive, be it on the TV or in our lives, perfect strangers. The automatic answer was 'no.' If I had ever told the truth, he would have been twisted with insecurity and it would have come back on me. It wasn't worth the hassle.

Our sex life got more and more detached, less intimate to say the least (dad you may want to skip this chapter!) He was obsessed with sex, he talked about it constantly. He told me many stories of previous partners, in far more detail than I ever wanted to hear. He would show me places of interest as we passed in the car, not historical landmarks, no. Places he had had sex. A window of an office, for example. You get the idea. To say he had been married for 13 years before he met me, he had certainly racked up the numbers.

He would often mention hookers, always joking of course. Once he encouraged me to go to a club which was right opposite our local. I had always been open minded, and we had been to clubs together in the past in the UK which were more welcoming, more like a sleazy working men's club but the people were generally non-threatening and friendly. This was different. I didn't like it, it was false, all they wanted was money. One girl asked me to buy her a drink, so I reluctantly agreed, assuming that was just normal. Five minutes later a bottle of champagne arrived, and I was handed the bill. I sent it back. What a piss take. I insisted we left.

Not surprisingly, he watched porn, a lot. Often 2-3 times a day. I never had an issue with porn years ago and felt a small amount was healthy if enjoyed in the right way, and privately. He would go upstairs and watch porn when his son was at home, telling me to make sure he didn't go in the bedroom.

However, in more recent years it was not only something he used by himself every day, but when we were in bed, together. He could no longer have sex without using it, sometimes on the TV in the bedroom but more often, and far worse, on the laptop, laid on his chest so that he couldn't even see me, only what was happening on the screen in front of him. I was merely taking the place of a blow-up doll at this point. I had got to the stage in my mind where I was shut off to it. I allowed him to do it. It kept him quiet for a bit longer. If I refused, I would have more silent treatment to look forward to. In his mind I was his wife, which meant I should fulfil his needs at all costs, at any time he felt like it. My needs, however, were ignored and unimportant.

His addiction to porn didn't help his jealousy. He would give examples of real-life scenarios but from a pornographic point of view. If I went to the office for the day to work, he would imagine a sex scene, with me over my boss's desk. Everything was a fantasy in his head, and he was starting to blur the lines between that and reality. He would tell me he was a realist, and that's what people did, I was being naïve if I thought otherwise.

He would now and again tell me had had ordered a gift for me online; at first, I would be curious, hoping for something nice, but it was always sex toys or slutty underwear. They usually remained in the packaging. I didn't want them. This would cause further anger from him. He would often tell our friends and people in the pub that we didn't have sex anymore. It was embarrassing and humiliating for everyone, I didn't understand what he was trying to achieve. Sympathy for himself? Who knows.

As a result, I didn't have any real desire to be intimate with him. He never kissed me or showed affection, simple things which could have made a difference. It was cold, clinical, and made me feel inadequate and unloved.

Surprisingly, a narcissist has extremely low self-esteem behind the charming, confident exterior. Everything about a narcissist is about them, but behind the façade they fear rejection, humiliation, defeat. Deep down they are frightened and fragile.

One thing that took me many years to realise, was that he was also a misogynist.

'Misogyny is the hatred of, contempt for, or prejudice against women or girls. Misogyny can be manifested in numerous ways, including social exclusion, sex discrimination, hostility, and male privilege ideas, belittling of women, violence against women, and sexual objectification of women. Misogynists treat women poorly

because they believe that they are above women in every way. A relationship with a misogynist comes with a host of problems, including the fact that it's neither healthy or fun if you're the woman in the relationship. Not all narcissists are misogynists, but most all misogynists are narcissists. (3)

It all made sense. The relationship he had with his mother, the contempt he held for her. His relationship with his daughter was a constant battle for years. He was overly critical of her, he would put her down, ask her why she wasn't more like her brother. She was very similar to him in a lot of ways, but he used this against her, seeing traits in her that he clearly didn't see in himself. As a result, she would rebel, push back. She craved his acceptance, his approval, but it was never forthcoming. I doubt she knew what a narcissist was at the time, but she did what she needed to, she cut him off at times, blocking his hurt towards her.

His objectification of women was also a clear-cut sign. To him, they were objects, to be either desired or dismissed. He was a flirt with the attractive ones, of course.

Usually in front of me, as if to say, 'look how attractive all these women find me, I could have them if I wanted them'. The porn fixation, the desire for me to get plastic surgery, it all made sense.

If he ever knew personal details of my friends; for example if they had ever confided him or told him anything about their past, he would hang on to the bare facts, and embellish them, always to create an image of being promiscuous, disloyal, a whore. He enjoyed recounting their tales to others, painting himself as a saint in the process.

It was the most hypocritical thing that I had ever witnessed. He would show disgust, distaste for these women who had perhaps been unfaithful to partners, or who were free spirited when growing up. No mention of the fact that he had repeatedly been unfaithful to his wife, a fact I found out many years later. No, that was justified, the marriage was already over. He couldn't see the irony in these bold statements. In his mind, women were money grabbing whores until proved otherwise. He decided I was no exception. If we ever discussed child maintenance after the split, he would scornfully tell me that I didn't need the money, that he wasn't going to give me anything. He was totally missing the point of what child maintenance was actually for.

If we went shopping, he would refuse to carry any bags. Not that I expected him to, I wasn't that old fashioned. But he would do it deliberately, often quoting the phrase "You women wanted equal rights, now you have them. Why should I help you?" His inability to do any DIY. He knew it was a weakness but turned it around and made me do it all, when I knew deep down it made him feel weak with inadequacy. He would joke about the car I chose to buy, calling it 'shit' and a 'heap' while he lorded around in his superior vehicle. That was, until it got stolen. Suddenly he needed the 'heap' and told me I needed to give it to him, he couldn't be expected to be without a car; but I could, obviously. No thought of how I would get our son to school if I was without a vehicle, no. All about his needs and wants.

Work was another factor. He would tell me his job was more important than mine and behave accordingly. If he was on a conference call at home, I would be told to make sure there was complete silence. I couldn't move around the house, couldn't do anything that even made a whisper of noise. If I did, I would be glared at. On the contrary if I was on a call, he would put the kettle on, play a video on his phone, put the TV on. If I ever said anything, he would say that it was fine because my call was insignificant, the people I worked with were stupid and didn't matter enough.

Over the last few years, women started to play a much more pivotal role in society. We were claiming our place and excelling at being treated as equals. He had a major issue with this, in particular when it came to sport. Women playing football? He was disgusted how they could be given so much airtime for their efforts Rugby? Even worse, that was a man's game. If a female was commentating on a football or rugby game, he would turn the channel over. He didn't believe they had the right to be doing that, what did they know about sport? It was unacceptable to him.

If women were employed in jobs such as the prison service or police force, he would find it laughable and say there was no way they could do a job like that, they were physically inferior, not capable of looking after themselves.

Many says he would say 'I hate the world.' He was rarely content, never happy and always thinking life could be better or that he needed to achieve more. His Facebook posts would often reflect the opposite of this, however. Selfies of himself, sat in the sunshine, with a drink. Pictures of us as a family, on the beach, in the pub, on a boat trip.

He wanted people to think we had the perfect life, to be envious of what we had achieved. He loved it when people commented that they were jealous, that he had 'done well' to be living the dream. Little did they know those happy days were few and far between. I used to fantasise about posting my own stories, videos of him paralytic, screenshots of his rants on text, images of me crying. Then the world would have really known.

He was talented in his job and initially moved up the ranks due to his skills. Slowly his arrogance in his job became a problem. He would make it clear to his superiors that he knew more than they gave him credit for. He would complain to colleagues and bosses that he was underpaid for his knowledge and that he should be given more. He pushed and pushed for superiority. This eventually led to contracts not being renewed, even terminated early. This only made everything worse, moving from role to role trying to find the place he could be who he believed he should be.

Nobody was giving him the pedestal he so craved, they were all wrong, they didn't understand him or see his true potential, he felt. His frustration only made the problem worse. People didn't want to work with him as he was difficult, aggressive. The only ones he ever forged reasonable working relationships with, were ex-military. With them he felt like he was accepted, understood. And for them he didn't feel the need to impress them so much. It was like he sensed they would see through any bullshit.

Most mornings in the last few years I felt like I was walking on eggshells. I never knew what mood he would wake up in and whichever it was, would form the mood for the day. If he woke up jealous and suspicious the day was ruined from the off. All day I would be conscious of every word that came out of my mouth. If he woke up cheerful and positive, we would have a great day. My anxiety was off the charts waiting for this daily roll of the dice. I tried to be strong, I tried to push back on those bad mornings, but it was impossible. His mood was so powerful and all-consuming that I was trapped in a spider's web, I couldn't be freed from it. Some days it took all the energy I had to get through the day without crying. My soul was being destroyed, piece by piece and I didn't recognise the person I was becoming. I felt immense shame that I had allowed myself to be treated like this. I couldn't tell anybody; they would think I was weak. My friend from the honeymoon was the only one to ever say to me 'You need to put your big girl pants on.' I couldn't. It was too terrifying.

Chapter Ten

2021

He went back to the UK in June for a few days to work. Peace and quiet, even if only short lived. He started sending me photos of houses in the UK. For the first time since 2016, he seemed to be considering going back. I was surprised, but fine with that, overjoyed actually. I missed my friends and mostly, my dad. He was 74 now and lockdown had kept us apart for longer than we had ever experienced. I told him I would be open to the idea of returning. When he got home, we discussed it at length and eventually decided to go for it. We began to look for a house and a school for our son. Our jobs were both remote so that was easy, nothing would change.

A month before we moved back, there was an incident. I'll refer to it as 'life saving number 2.'

We had been out in the afternoon with friends for lunch. He was drinking vodka and orange, unusual for him but he had started drinking vodka for the last week. I could tell when we left the restaurant he had already had too much. We called at our local pub but didn't stay long. He was loud and annoying, and I just wanted to be at home. The usual scenario unfolded. He carried on drinking at home, and I went to bed. At one point I went downstairs for a drink and could see he was drinking vodka neat. I asked him why and he said she had run out of orange juice. I asked him to stop drinking and he ignored me.

As usual, the music started. Midnight, 1am, 2am it continued. Louder and louder. I repeatedly went downstairs and asked him to turn it down. At one point I unplugged the speaker. It finally got too much for me. I was furious. Our son had got into bed with me and I went downstairs again. This time I was screaming at him. I don't remember what I said. I felt hysterical. I went back upstairs and it fell quiet. Thank god.

I heard a smash of glass and more silence. Then, he shouted my name. I knew something was wrong. He wouldn't usually ask for my help unless he really needed it. I told my son to stay where he was. I went downstairs, my stomach filled with dread. All I could see was blood all over the patio. Lots of it. The broken gin glass in front of him and blood cascading from his palm. The blood was on the walls, the chairs, table, even the swimming pool. It looked like a murder scene. I quickly grabbed an old sheet and made a tourniquet. He was clammy and grey, and I genuinely thought he was going to bleed out. I called the ambulance, but they weren't interested. Even less so when they asked if he had been drinking. They were busy, it could be hours. He didn't even know what day it was and was slipping in and out of consciousness.

Eventually he crawled upstairs. The bleeding had slowed. He got into the shower and promptly collapsed. He came around and shouted at me for trying to call for the ambulance. In the end I called the emergency services back and told them he was refusing to go to hospital even if they did turn up. He got into bed, and I sat up all night to make sure he didn't bleed any more or die.

The next day, he was actually shocked when he saw the patio. For once he was humble and apologetic. But I was still the one who spent an entire morning cleaning blood from our beautiful villa terrace. That day I threw all of the alcohol out of the house and announced that drinking was no longer allowed at home. It was quickly forgotten. By him, at least. I was remaining positive that in less than a month we would be back in the UK and close to friends and family. It kept me going.

Chapter Eleven

Taking care of business

Business was never his strong point. He had a few companies in the past, as his industry required him to be self-employed. Admin wasn't his thing either. I was appointed as secretary for both and was expected to run the whole process. He generally didn't open any mail, both business and personal. Speeding tickets would arrive and they would be ignored, and he would hope for the best.

With the first company he had ignored an important letter from the bank to say he needed to withdraw any funds by a certain date, or it would be taken by Companies House as the company had been dissolved along with the business bank account and was therefore unable to be kept open any longer. As a result, we lost £12,000 and had no money for months. On that day I got the keys for our new house. Luckily, we had already paid the rent but had nothing else. I had to borrow 50 euros from the sympathetic letting agent who insisted we use it to buy food and essentials for a few days. To this day he still blames the bank rather than taking responsibility for his own actions.

He opened a new company and yet again I was told to deal with all the finances. He had a strange way of thinking how a company should work financially and constantly wanted to withdraw as much money as he could out of the account. I repeatedly told him it doesn't work like that and that we would end up with a huge bill. He told me that the accountant I was using was clearly shit and didn't know what they were talking about, and it would be fine. We had to register for VAT due to the income of the business, which we were then supposed to pay directly back to HMRC. When lockdown happened, he instructed me not to pay it, to keep hold of it. Eventually I gave up trying to explain the consequences of using the business account as personal expenses. He knew better. When I first left him in March 2022, I told him I wanted out of the business. It was causing me unnecessary stress and I needed him to take over the full control and run it the way he believed it should be run. He turned it around on me and accused me of cutting more ties for the day I inevitably left him. He was half right.

As predicted, he didn't take over the control at all and let the business run into the ground. To this day he now has a large unpaid debt which he publicly blames me for, claiming that I kept him in the dark and didn't fulfil the role he had conveniently created for me.

Chapter Twelve

Back in the UK

We moved back home in September 2021. He went ahead a month before me, to arrange a vehicle. The house was already secured. As usual I was left to tie up everything at the other end and take on all the stress of moving while he socialised and caught up with his mates. But I knew if he was with me the stress would have been tenfold. At least this way I could get everything sorted in my own way without his criticism that I hadn't packed things correctly and so on.

He didn't say goodbye to anybody. He had pretty much managed to fall out with everyone he had previously considered a 'friend.' People were sick of his attitude, his inability to control his temper when drunk, or his temper when playing golf. As always, he took the higher ground, claiming that people misunderstood him. It was their problem, he hadn't done anything wrong, in his head. There were arguments, near fights, which I only found out about sometime later.

One of his closest friends was a guy I called Irish Ian. They had got on well for months and played a lot of golf together, drank together. One afternoon they had been out together, and I had met up with them. He was wasted and being horrible and annoying, so I ended up walking out of our friend Darren's bar and getting a taxi home. I don't remember what time he staggered in. The next morning, he looked sheepish. He told me thought they may have fallen out, but he didn't remember the details. He checked his phone for messages and sent Ian a message apologising for whatever he may have done. No response.

Later that day I had a message from a friend of Ian's, saying that his golf clubs and a few other things were at our house and a car would be sent to collect them. Basically, Ian didn't want anything to do with him ever again. What the hell had happened? I showed him the message and he was taken aback; he couldn't remember a thing. I replied to the friend to try and find out what had happened but no, she wasn't giving anything up. She was quite rude to me, and I left it at that. Yet another friend he had manage to piss off. At first, he seemed quite upset, and I actually felt sorry for him at first. It seemed so harsh no matter what he had done, surely, he had only said something inappropriate, and Ian had a tough hide, it must have been really bad to have come to this.

His upset quickly turned to dismissiveness and irritation, and it was barely mentioned again. It was a shame for all of us. Not only was it about the two of them but we were a group of friends – two married guys and Ian's close friend, an older lady who he called 'mum' after his own mother had passed away. I was close to them all and we socialised weekly, sometimes more. Suddenly we were out of the gang. I was unfortunately a victim of whatever trouble he had caused so now I had lost my friends too. I was so frustrated and confused, the not knowing why was the worst thing, but I had to soldier on. My son was really sad as he was also close to them all, especially Ian, who had taught him to play pool.

My situation abroad was generally somewhat different when it came to friends. I had lots of them, and I would miss many people out there when we left. I spent the last week meeting up with as many people as I could before my son, and I flew back to England. That's between packing up and shipping our entire worldly belongings, that is. One thing remained unresolved before we left, which was our car, which we leased through our bank. I had tried to return it several times before we left but it was proving difficult. As is so often the case when you live abroad, the language barrier makes things a lot more difficult, especially when it comes to admin or paperwork. The car was in my name despite us having a joint account, so he wasn't interested in helping me sort it before he left. He would joke that it was my problem if it wasn't sorted. Add it to the list, I thought. Before I left, I handed the keys to my closest friend, and we agreed to sort it after I had gone home.

God, it was so good to be home. I couldn't wait to see everyone. The area we moved to was green, we had hills, we had cows and sheep. We had plants and trees. To me it was heaven. It was autumn and one of the most beautiful seasons in the UK as the leaves are turning vivid shades of gold, orange and red. I could breathe. This is where I belonged. Gone were the cockroaches, the constant heat where you feel like you spend your life covered in sweat and sun cream, sliding around on white plastic chairs, drinking cheap booze. I never realised how much I had missed the UK until then.

We spent lots of time visiting friends and family that we hadn't seen since the wedding. It felt like a honeymoon period almost. Certainly, better than the last one, anyway. We socialised regularly as we always did, got to know the local pubs and where we liked, where we didn't like. My best friend lived in the same village, which was a huge bonus, I never felt alone at first knowing I had her there for support, and everyone else we were close to only lived an hour or so away. It was a comforting feeling.

I couldn't wait to go on girlie nights, lunches, days out with my friends. It had been years. He even seemed excited for me too and said he was happy that I had my old friends back near me.

However as with any honeymoon, this didn't last. I didn't go on any girlie nights out. I rarely went for lunch without him. If I suggested something with my friend, he would respond almost with outrage that I wanted to be away from him and my son. What was he supposed to do if I went out? He couldn't stay at home on his own! So, I didn't plan anything. If my friend invited me to anything I would have to make an excuse as to why I couldn't go. She wasn't stupid, she knew how it was and left me to it.

His behaviour changed if we socialised with others. He would sulk if he wasn't the main topic or storyteller in the conversation and he would repeatedly push his empty glass towards me and tell me to go to the bar, especially if I was in the middle of a conversation that didn't involve him.

Once I had gone to the bar he would watch me like a hawk, see if I was chatting to anyone. It was like having a three-year-old with me, and it was embarrassing. If there was a male with us, a friend, a friend's husband, whatever - he would accuse me of them making too much eye contact with me and belittling him by not addressing him directly or including him enough in conversation.

One night he actually woke me up from my sleep to ask me who I was texting. He said he could hear my fingers tapping at phone. I was asleep, he was utterly delusional. In the morning, he woke me up early, his phone screen thrust into my face. 'Who's this? He's on your friends list on Facebook. Did you go out with him?'

One weekend one of his best friends came to stay. He is a physiotherapist and was talking to me about a new muscular technique. He offered to try it on me. My first reaction was to refuse as I already knew *He* would have an issue with it, even though he had known this guy his whole life. I asked him to come in the room with us, more for my benefit than his as I could already feel an accusation brewing. He said he wasn't interested so my son sat and watched while his friend showed me the technique. No surprise that months later he was still talking about it. I asked why he didn't trust even his best friend, or me for that matter. He would always say that he didn't trust anyone, including him. I thought it was desperately sad that he would feel like that even about his closest friends. I have a favourite phrase that suited this scenario perfectly. 'It takes one to know one.'

Chapter Thirteen

The Silent Treatment

This was the worst part for me. I found it torturous. It could go on for days, and not only would he ignore me, but my son would be ignored too. I would sit and cry in our bedroom, hiding my emotions from my son and him. I didn't want him to know he was getting to me.

It would be triggered by anything. Maybe I had a conversation in a pub and didn't include him. Maybe I went shopping and didn't take him. If I went into the office and wore make-up, he would ask why I was making a special effort. I would get home later that day to the inevitable silence. I'm the sort of person who prefers to talk things though and to clear the air. He isn't.

Silent treatment is a psychological form of abuse. It changes the daylight into a sinister cloak of fear. Daily tasks are harder and sad. Conversation with friends and family is tense and you don't want to speak to anyone as the cloak of fear and sadness is so heavy it weighs you down. You long for night-time for the escape of sleep although dreading the cold unwelcoming bed. It was a relief when he chose to sleep in the spare room as at least the room was free of tension.

I would wake up the next day hoping that the switch would have flicked back. Sometimes it would have, and things would return to normal. Mostly it would continue. I would ask him to stop and talk to me, but he would claim that nothing was wrong, and he was acting fine. He would try and make me think it was my issue. Eventually when he was ready to be normal again, or usually if he needed me for something or needed me to be his sounding board after a bad day at work, he would start talking to me as if nothing had happened. For some reason I never resisted and allowed the normality to come back, as the relief of being accepted by him again was overwhelming. It sounds so pathetic when I even type this, but that's how it was. I was controlled by everything he did and said, and I didn't see it fully.

Chapter Fourteen

Once bitten, twice shy

The first time I left was in March 2022. We had just come back from a really enjoyable family trip to Wales where we had visited his family. This was another group of people who never really saw the controlling side, he was always lovely and sociable, charming when we were with them. His mood was good.

We met my best friend in the local pub when we got home and had a Sunday roast. He wanted to go home straight after, but I was enjoying myself and wanted to stay, though as usual I did as he wanted, and we drove home. In the car he suggested if I wanted to, I could go back after I had dropped him off. I was surprised at the suggestion as it was out of character for him. I agreed but said I would take my son with me as it meant we could walk to school the next morning as she lived close by. He said fine. I knew he wasn't fine, but I went anyway, it felt like my parents had allowed me out for the first time as a teenager.

I had a lovely relaxing evening with her, listening to old 90's tunes, reminiscing about our childhood. I messaged him a couple of times to which I only received one-word responses and went to bed around 10.45pm.

The next morning after my son had been dropped off at school, I drove home. He was frosty to say the least and when I asked what was wrong, he accused me of staying up late, keeping my son up late, and not messaging him enough. I told him that was ridiculous, but he went on and on. Something in me snapped. I changed my clothes and went for a run. I needed to breathe, to release what was bubbling away inside of me. When I got back it was more of the same. Over and over. I packed a bag and told him I was going to go back to my friends for the night as I couldn't cope with his behaviour anymore, and I had done nothing wrong; all I had done was spend the evening with my son and best friend. I realised he was getting to a point where couldn't do anything without me and it was starting to feel like complete dependence, both practical and emotional. I needed to get out. Now.

Within an hour I had a call from a close mutual friend- he was already telling people I left him, claiming he had no idea why. The victim came out quicker than I expected.

I stayed there for 10 days. I felt free. In my heart I knew this was what I should have done a long time ago. He hounded me for those 10 days. One day he would accept it was over and start talking about dividing the house or other practical affairs. Then he would turn nasty, accusing me of taking all the money out of the business account, that I was leaving him and ripping him off too, misinterpreting a text message he had received from the bank. The next minute he would beg me to come home, he loved me and couldn't live without me. I was his world.

I went to my dad's house for a couple of days. It was a sanctuary, a place where I felt safe and loved and not under scrutiny. On the Saturday night my son and I were asleep. I heard my dad open our bedroom door and he said he had just been on the phone to my husband. Apparently, we had been burgled. Interesting. He had been out at the pub with his eldest son and think they disturbed the thieves when they returned. They hadn't taken anything except his watch and his sons car keys. When I spoke to him, he shouted at me for not answering the phone when he had called me first. I had been asleep, and he didn't even believe me. He accused me of not being interested in what had happened. He went and bought a Ring doorbell, and several cameras, placing them all over the grounds of the house.

The following Monday I had lunch with my friend and her boyfriend and his parents at a local pub. Whilst waiting for the food to arrive, he video called me. I considered ignoring the call but knew it would cause more problems. I answered it, moving to a communal area away from our table to the inevitable question of 'where are you?' I told him. Should be no big issue. He wanted me to look at some fingerprints on the wardrobe which may link to the burglary. It was a brief chat. After I had put the phone down, he messaged me and asked why he could hear a male voice in the background. Was he being serious? I was stood in a busy pub, with people constantly walking past. He didn't believe me. I was past caring.

The days rolled by and eventually, after his pleading, I gave in and agreed to go home. He promised he would get an appointment to see a counsellor and would work on some of his issues. I believed he wanted to try so I felt like I should give him one more opportunity, especially for the sake of our son. I went home.

The first day back, he invited his eldest son and friend to stay, believing it would lighten the air and make it less pressure for my return. I was happy with that; I was already feeling uneasy about going back. We went out for a few drinks, and I started to relax a little. Conversation flowed easily as a group. When we got home, I was accused of dominating the conversation about my online business, and the friend who had come along was giving me too much attention about it, as he was interested in it and asked me a lot of questions. Back was the spoilt child who wanted all the focus to be on him. Not the best start. The friend in question actually called him out on it and told him how it was. He swallowed it and didn't mention it again.

The next two months was an ongoing battle between him showing he was making an effort and struggling to control his emotions. He was reading the self-help books, talking about his feelings. But even that was backfiring. He was pushing me to read them too, telling me that I needed to deal with 'my issues' too because he didn't really believe deep down that any of this was about him. He said I needed to accept responsibility for my own actions too.

I spoke to him about a psychological phobia called *'Fear of abandonment.'* A common anxiety experienced from those who had experienced parental separation. I knew that some of the behaviour he exhibited linked to this. It was no surprise to me that *Good Will Hunting* was his favourite film, and the only film I knew which could provoke an emotional response from him.

The jealousy of those around me, the dependency, the insecurity. There were days when he would look at me with a sad face and say, 'Please don't leave me.' It was a vulnerable side I didn't see often, and I hoped that explaining some of this to him would help him understand. I gave him some examples of his recent behaviour and linked it to this fear. He seemed to understand, to grasp the connection I was making. It felt like a momentary breakthrough. I wanted him to understand this himself, not for me to tell him what was wrong. I would explain that he needed to understand his behaviour before trying to jump into any kind of marriage counselling. I was a big believer that people need to be happy in their own skin before being able to be happy in a relationship.

As quickly as we made new ground, we lost it. He couldn't fight the battle in his own head for long enough to think logically. Within minutes any conversation would turn into accusations about what I had been getting up to behind his back in those 10 days I spent away from him, despite the fact my son was with me. I realised that the separation had only made things worse. He simply didn't trust me, despite 10 years of loyalty and devotion to him. I was never going to win, never going to be able to help him, if he couldn't accept his fault in his actions.

His obsession with my social media accounts increased, he would scroll through my Instagram profile constantly, asking who people were who followed me. He showed a sudden interest in my business and said I was leaving him out of it, and he should be part of it all. I would explain that I had had the business for 4 years, had grown it myself and it was my own path. He had never been interested before but suddenly was even seeing that as a threat to 'us.' All I wanted from him was a little support, to be proud of my success and encourage me to move forward.

He did not accept this at all and said it was wrong of me to want a part of my life or career that was only for me. It was selfish of me. He accused me of hiding money from him that I had earned through the business which had never been the case. Any money I earnt was used to fund our lifestyle, buy things for the house and a tidy 12k for the wedding that I had paid.

He was threatened by my success, my ambition and drive. He believed he was becoming less important to me, that my focus was elsewhere. He thought I would get rich and then leave him. His insecurity was suffocating me, breath by breath.

One day I had a reprieve as he was needed in the office. I agreed to drop him off at the train station and pick him up later. I spent the day created a social media video for my business which I had mentioned to him earlier. The video took a lot longer than I thought, and we had messaged briefly through the day. When I picked him up that evening, I could tell as soon as he got in the car that something was wrong. I asked him and he said nothing. My temper was becoming shorter and shorter by the day, and I told him to tell me immediately what was wrong and not give me the usual silent treatment. He told me that I had not messaged him enough. That I had obviously prioritised my business over him. I was enraged. There's neediness and just plain pathetic, I thought. He had been at work the whole day, yet I was the one off radar? On this occasion, I was the one giving the silent treatment. I couldn't find the words.

One weekend he went to York on a stag night on the Friday. The next morning, we sent a few messages back and forth and I told him to let me know when he wanted picking up from the train station. At 10am he sent me a photograph of a pint of lager in a pub somewhere. By midday I hadn't heard from him, so I called him. He had got as far as Sheffield and was now in a pub next to the station. Great. I already knew how this day would go. I took my son to the park, wondering how much of my day would be spent waiting for him to get back so we could do something as a family. The trains back home were every hour.

Each hour I would get a message to say he had missed the train. This went on and on. By about 4pm I decided to have a drink at the pub which was next to the park. I felt defiant, stubborn for once. Why should I sit there all day like an idiot, with no plans apart from waiting for him? He was happy to leave me hanging.

I messaged him to say I was now having a drink after waiting all day for him to come home. His tone automatically changed. Accusing, abrupt. Sarcastic. I knew then he wouldn't be coming home any time soon. It got to about 6pm and he sent me a photo of himself in a local pub, but in a village 3 miles away from me. This meant not only had he finally managed to catch a train, but instead of getting off at our stop, he had stayed on to go to the pub he wanted. This irritated me. I told him he would need to get a bus now. Personally, I felt it was reasonable and I know he would have done the same if it had been the other way around. His messages were becoming more illegible, and I knew he was wasted, as usual. Sarcastic comments saying he assumed I wouldn't pick him up and now he was stranded. He then went offline for the rest of the night. Not a word. As usual, I sat at home waiting for the inevitable dramatic entrance. At 10pm I gave up and went to bed, my stomach twisting with anxiety. I heard shouting outside at 11pm. I ran downstairs and found him in the greenhouse, pissing all over my new tomato plants that my dad had bought and planted for me a week earlier for my birthday.

I can't even explain the rage I felt inside. I pulled him out of the greenhouse, shouting at him and went to bed, furious. He slept in the spare room after keeping me awake until 2am, singing and shouting in the garden with the usual loud music on.

The next morning, I stupidly expected an apology, how silly of me. I made him a cup of tea as normal, and he blanked me. He was furious with me. He said I had 'fucked him off' and left him stranded. I'd abandoned him and not offered a lift. I was astounded. I felt like I had been punched in the stomach. Even my son turned round and said to me 'mum, how can he be mad at you? It was all his fault!'

He left the house, no word of where to. I remember sitting on the bed, tears of rage and frustration pouring down my face. I was as low as I could get. I felt like I was in a mental prison, trapped with no way out. I hated what he was doing to me, turning me into a pathetic mess, unable to stand up to him or for myself. This was my *husband*. A marriage was supposed to have love, respect, trust. I felt none of those things. He would tell me he loved me, but it wasn't how love should be. Not to me. It was love based on control, on coercion. I didn't know what to do.

After hours of vile messages about how I had allegedly 'treated' him, he admitted he had lost his bag the night before and was out looking for it. I knew that meant he would be in the pub. He did apologise about the plants.

It got to 1.30pm and he was still out. He sent me a message asking what was for tea.

At 1.35pm he sent me a random screenshot of a girl I used to work with, asking who she is as she had popped up on 'people you should know' on Facebook. I told him who she was. His reply? 'I'd fuck her.' Lovely.

At 3pm he asked me to come to the pub. The booze had now softened his anger and his mood had switched. My son and I went, reluctantly. I was still raging but need a conclusion and for this sadness and anger to be taken away from me.

We didn't stay long. I was on edge and couldn't just pretend I was ok for once. Something in me had changed. We ended up arguing in the pub and I took my son home. We had a blazing argument in the garden where he said things to me too upsetting to repeat. I was done. The last straw was finding out my son had text his older brother to say we were arguing, and he didn't know what to do. He was scared. This snapped him into some sort of reality and was suddenly remorseful.

The next day was a complete shift in behaviour. Loving messages while I was at the office, the works. Telling me to have a good day, saying he was proud of me. It was exhausting but I carried on. What other choice did I have?

A week later he brought it up again on text, completely out of the blue. He said he was still angry and that I had 'zero interest' in picking him up. It started a whole day of arguments back and forth on the phone. I felt weak and ready to give up. Even when he was in the wrong, he could always find an angle to terrorise me over it for months, sometimes years on end the same accusations would come out at the most unexpected times.

Chapter Fifteen

Gaslighting

'Narcissistic gaslighting doesn't differ from normal gaslighting, but it may be used for slightly different manipulative purposes. For instance, a narcissist might use these tactics to preserve or protect their ego, keep others from challenging them, or maintain a sense of superiority over others.' (3)

There are so many ways that a narcissist can demonstrate gaslighting:

Citing Past Mistakes You've Made

A common gaslighting technique narcissists use involves undermining or questioning your credibility by pointing out past mistakes you've made. By always bringing up these mistakes, they undermine your confidence in your abilities while providing an excuse for why they can't trust you. They are also known to select mistakes you feel especially ashamed of, since these are more likely to trigger you.

Pulling the 'You're Crazy' Card

Accusing someone of being 'crazy' or emotionally or mentally unstable is common tactic narcissists use. They might directly accuse you of being crazy, psychotic, or mentally ill, or they may just suggest it by using gaslighting phrases like, 'You might want to get your meds adjusted.' If you get upset or angry, they may use your reaction as further 'proof' that you're unstable.

Questioning Your Memory

Another gaslighting example is to call your memory into question and suggest you're mixing up your facts or misremembering something. Narcissistic gaslighting examples of this tactic include suggesting you're 'confused,' 'mixed up' or 'misremembering.' Alternatively, they may take the opposite approach, saying something like, 'I have no memory of that' or, 'I don't know what you're talking about.'

Outright Denial of the Facts

Denial is another example of narcissistic gaslighting; it includes a blatant denial of facts. For example, gaslighting narcissists may use phrases like, 'That never happened' or, 'You're imagining things.' They may outright deny any wrongdoing by saying things like, 'I would never do something like that.'

Playing the Good Guy

Narcissistic gaslighters often want to play the good guy in every situation, painting themselves as the hero of every story. One tactic involves pretending they're the only ones who really love and care about you, while pointing out ways others have let you down or betrayed you.

Shifting Blame to Avoid Accountability

A narcissist rarely takes responsibility for their mistakes and is more likely to change the facts and shift blame onto others. For example, they might swear that a malicious act of revenge was accidental or purely coincidental. They may also shift the blame by accusing you or someone else of doing something wrong or provoking them, instead of owning up to their actions.

Projecting Their Faults onto You

Projecting personal faults is a classic form of gaslighting designed to prevent people from being able to call them out for their shortcomings. An example of projection is accusing *you* of being narcissistic or self-centred, or saying you care too much about what others think of you. This kind of projection is a common way that narcissists respond to an ego threat.

Pretending to Have Allies

Narcissists often form alliances with others to attack and discredit a person, or just pretend that others agree with them even when they don't. This triangulation tactic is designed to make you feel more isolated, while also causing you to question yourself. Examples of how narcissists use pretend alliances to gaslight others are claiming that 'everyone' or certain people have said negative things behind your back.

Using Indignant Outrage

Narcissistic rage or indignant anger is triggered when a narcissist's ego is threatened or challenged. This defensive form of anger aims to shut down anyone who is challenging the narcissist. They also want to portray themselves as the victim. Examples are phrases like, 'How dare you accuse me of something like that!' or, 'I won't stand for this kind of treatment!'

Comparing You to Others

Another tactic narcissistic gaslighters use is to compare you to other people in ways that make you feel inadequate. This tactic is designed to undermine your confidence and self-esteem while pitting you against others. Examples include gaslighting phrases like 'You should ask ____ for help since they're a lot better at it than you' or, 'I wish you were more like ____.'

Accusing You of Being Too Sensitive

Another common form of narcissistic gaslighting is accusing someone of being overly emotional or sensitive. By doing so, the narcissist suggests the person's emotions prevent them from being able to see a situation clearly. By saying things like, 'You're too emotional' or 'You take things too personally,' they can avoid being held accountable for hurtful things they say or do.

Feigning Concern for Your Wellbeing

Another form of gaslighting narcissists use is pretending to care or be concerned about someone as a back-handed way of suggesting they're irrational, crazy, or unstable. Feigned concern is a passive aggressive tactic that appears to be kind but is designed to undermine someone's credibility. Examples include asking repeatedly if you're feeling OK or if you've been sleeping enough.

Using Your Own Words Against You

Another gaslighting trick used by narcissists is to use your own words against you, often by taking them out of context or twisting their meaning. Weaponising things you've said in the past is a way to suggest you're contradicting yourself or being hypocritical. Gaslighting phrases like, 'Like you always say…' 'I thought you said….' or, 'You were the one who suggested…' are examples of this.

Inverting the Truth

Inverting (or reversing) the truth is another form of gaslighting. Inversion states the opposite of the truth, like accusing someone else of saying or doing the things they said or did. They may also refer to abusive or controlling behaviour as acts of love. Because it's so blatant, inverting the truth can make people doubt and question themselves more than subtler forms of gaslighting.

Trivializing What Matters to You

Narcissists often trivialize things that are important or significant to someone else. For example, they may undermine a person's passion or career by referring to it as a 'hobby.' They may also trivialize painful past experiences by comparing them to other, more serious or traumatic experiences.

Saying Your Opinions Don't Count

Invalidation is a form of gaslighting that directly discredits what someone else thinks or feels. Saying that your opinion doesn't count because you don't know enough about a subject is a form of gaslighting designed to silence your opinions. Narcissists are most likely to use this tactic when your opinion differs from their own, which they see as a direct threat, insult, or challenge. (3)

Does any of that sound familiar? It sure does to me.

On every occasion that we argued, or he treated me badly he would always blame me. I was the one who made him act that way. I provoked him, pushed him into reacting badly and therefore he felt justified to treat me like first as it was a direct response. It's hard sometimes not to believe this may be true. Maybe it was me?

If an argument was going in a direction that meant he couldn't win or he couldn't justify his actions, he would stonewall me.

'Stonewalling involves refusing to communicate with another person and withdrawing from the conversation to create distance between the individual and their partner. Intentionally shutting down during an argument, also known as the silent treatment, can be hurtful, frustrating, and harmful to the relationship.

Stonewalling is broadly described by the following behaviours:

- A general discomfort in discussing feelings.
- Dismissing or minimising the other person's concerns.
- Refusing to respond to questions.
- Refusing to make eye contact or offer nonverbal communication cues.

- Walking away from discussions that cause stress.' (4)

In our case, it often meant he would leave the house to go to the pub or go into another room and not emerge for hours until he needed me for something and then all of a sudden everything was fine, and he would flick a switch and be nice again. I would try and try to get him to talk, to evaluate, to get it off his chest so we could move forward but I would be shut down immediately. It just wasn't an option.

One weekend we decided to spend some time at my dad's house with his partner, on the coast. A change of scenery, a chance to break out of those four walls for a change. We found out that another couple that we knew were also in the area that weekend. We arranged to meet up with them for the evening.

All was going well, conversation flowed, and we told them about our recent relationship issues and that we were trying to work things through. It felt good to share this so openly. However, things quickly went downhill. The men went to the bar together to get the next round of drinks. After about half an hour we wondered what was taking them so long. We could see them stood at the bar so assumed they were just engrossed in some one-to-one conversation. My friend's husband was ex-army so as always, they could relate to each other.

We had empty glasses now and lured them away from the bar to go to the next pub. We noticed then that their drunkenness had rapidly multiplied. They had been doing shots at the bar. Great.

We left the pub together, my friend and I at the front and the guys behind. We kept glancing back to make sure they were keeping pace. Then, they were gone. Vanished into thin air. We stopped walking and turned back. We had passed one pub so assumed they had maybe staggered into there and not bothered telling us. Nope, nowhere to be seen. We went back to the street and couldn't see them anywhere. Frustrated, we gave up and decided to grab a pizza nearby and try and get hold of them. Neither of them were answering their phones. It seemed to us a like a deliberate move to shake us off. We knew what they could be like when they were together. We got our pizza and headed back home, me to my dads and her to the bed and breakfast they were staying at.

I went to bed, but not to sleep. I had messaged him for hours now with no responses. Eventually, a call. So drunk I could barely understand what he was saying. He was lost and couldn't remember where my dad left. He sent a photo of himself at the pizza place. He was only down the road. I explained where to go, even sent him a map.

Another hour ticked by, still no sign. He was lost again. This went on for hours until I finally heard him stagger in after I had eventually fallen asleep, around 2am. He walked into the bedroom, and I think I recall saying something sarcastic like 'you found it then' He replied, 'Fuck you.' Nice. I went to sleep.

The next morning, I at least expected him to laugh it off, for us to verbally play back the nights events. No. He walked out of my dad's, to where I didn't know. He eventually came back. My dad and I were confused, what was he doing? We all went out for lunch, and I could tell he wasn't speaking to me. There was no way I was letting another weekend be ruined by the pathetic silent treatment.

He was being lovely to everyone else, jovial almost. But I was invisible. When I asked him what was wrong, he told me I had deliberately left him, made a choice to lose him so I could run away. I was astounded. Not this again.

We sat in the café and ordered some food. The mood was tense. I had pulled my dad to one side to explain what was happening. He shook his head and muttered 'he's an arsehole.' Nothing more. We were chatting between us at the table and the subject fell to the previous night. He started telling us that he was lost and was nowhere near my dad's place. I corrected him, I knew this wasn't the case.

He argued back, he said he had found a Premier Inn hotel and had an argument with the receptionist who refused to give him a room. I pointed out that the Premier Inn was 5 minutes' walk away. No, he said, it was a different one, I'm not stupid I would know if it was that one. I knew for a fact there was only one in town. I even showed him the map and the website which clearly showed only one. He wouldn't have it.

He then started going on and on that he had been so hungry because he hadn't eaten all night. Oh really? I thought to myself. Time to make him look stupid by showing evidence to the contrary. I showed him the photo he had sent me from the pizza place, complete with pizza. We all laughed at his mistake. He didn't. I had belittled him and made him look like an idiot. I had proved him wrong with cold hard facts. I was satisfied, and perhaps a little smug. I didn't actually care; he had managed to do a good enough job of that by himself.

Later we went for a walk just the two of us. We went to the bar at the Premier Inn where he realised that yes, this is where he was the night before. He went to the reception area and asked that an apology was made on his behalf to the night staff who he had been aggressive to.

I didn't get an apology.

I started to focus more on my health and fitness again and joined the local gym, paying the extra for a personal trainer. I was sick of him calling me fat and I needed to pull myself together and feel good about myself again. Not for his benefit but for my own. He took this as a sign that I was suddenly taking care of my appearance for someone else's benefit. To prove him otherwise, I encouraged him to join me.

He would spend the whole sessions telling the personal trainer that he was really fit a few years ago, and that he couldn't believe he was being shamed into doing pathetic exercises that he already knew how to do. He was an expert, no less. Luckily the PT didn't take offence to this as a slight on her professional training. I later found out her ex was a narcissist. She knew one when she saw one.

One day we were at the gym and there was one guy there also, a bodybuilder. Immediately, he was threatened. I didn't even speak to this guy, didn't really know him, but the battle lines were drawn. During our exercises he would stroke my arm, smack my arse. I felt sick with humiliation and with the blatant way he was marking his territory. It was so obvious. After we broke up he would claim that we were so happy, we were holding hands in the gym! Everything was lovely! No, no. He eventually accused me of having affairs with men at the gym, he was really grasping at straws now. I had even had to make sure I had a female personal trainer, if they had been male, my life would have been hell.

Back when we lived abroad, there had been one night where I had gone out for a drink with my friend after work. He was at home, and I didn't plan on being out long. We had a few drinks and it went straight to my head. She got a lift home at short notice, and I was then on my own. I wanted to finish my drink and was chatting to the owners of the bar. He text me to ask when I would be home and I told him I was setting off, with the full intention of leaving in a few minutes. The owners then bought me a drink, so I stayed to finish it. Nothing major as far as I was concerned and certainly the exact sort of thing he would have done without a second thought. I then walked home and felt a bit woozy due to the wine, so I went straight to bed.

For not only months, but years, he has accused me of something happening on the way home or at that bar. It was an uneventful evening and yet in his mind he has created the most outlandish scenarios in his head about it. Years later I would wake up in the morning and he would say to me 'What happened that night, you need to tell me.' I just couldn't find the words to tell him how ridiculous it was. I can probably count over 100 times that he had text me to say he was coming home and then turned up hours later, I certainly wasn't bringing that up with him in the future, he clearly couldn't handle it when the boot was on the other foot.

To my knowledge he has even contacted my friend recently trying to get information out of her. It is utterly pathetic.

Chapter Sixteen

Day one.

The date is burned into my brain. 9th of June. It had been a truly awful day. For a few days he had been hounding me about social media yet again. He had asked me if I ever had unwanted attention from guys or if I had ever been sent suggestive pictures or asked for them. I hadn't and I told him so. What I didn't know at the time was he had already seized an opportunity to go through my phone when I was in the garden. There was nothing to go on, apart from an old mutual friend who commented on one of my weight loss photos. It was banter and nothing more and he would have seen that I told this guy to piss off.

We had to go shopping for a suit that day for his friend's funeral, so we went to an out-of-town shopping centre. There were a few things I needed too and thought we could have lunch while our son was at school. It took almost two hours to get the suit sorted and when we left that particular shop, I was starving. I asked him if he wanted food. His mood had switched completely, and he was rolling his eyes when I mentioned I need to go to one shop for myself.

He opened a message on his phone, and someone had sent him a porn video. A load of squaddies and some famous young girl who I hadn't heard of. He proceeded to watch it whilst walking around the shopping centre. I asked him to stop which he seemed to enjoy. He made derogatory comments about the video to suggest it may have been something I would have done in my past. He knew I had been out with a couple of blokes who were ex-military and he never let it drop. His tone was loaded with venom, and he was goading me, pushing for a reaction. I left without both lunch and getting what shopping I needed. The disgust I felt towards him was building rapidly and I wanted to be away from this man. We drove home in silence, picked up our son and went to the local for a drink where we met my friend.

He had a look in his eyes I couldn't read. I had a problem with my contact lens and had to take it out, joking with him that he couldn't drink too much as I wouldn't be able to take over the driving responsibility. He said that was fine and he only wanted one anyway. After half an hour or so the switch flicked again. He ordered another double gin and tonic from the bar and told me he was getting pissed and I was driving. I told him we had discussed it and that I was down to sight in only one eye. I went to the bathroom, mainly to have a minute with myself. I could feel trouble brewing and I had the inevitable feeling of dread at the pit of my stomach. I took several deep breaths before returning to the table.

When I returned, I could tell he had been saying something about me to my friend that was derogatory. He kept mentioning Instagram, his eyes dancing with malice every time he said it, like he had a private joke with himself.

So, I was forced to drive home with only sight in one eye, with my child in the car. We didn't speak for the rest of the evening until we went to bed around 10pm. I asked him what he had spoken to my friend about and what the hell his problem was. He told me I was a liar and that he had already been through my phone and that I clearly speak to men. I explained that the only men I spoke to were clients and they were always professional conversations. But the trigger was flicked in me. The fact he had violated my privacy and not for the first time, was that last straw.

From somewhere deep within, I found my voice, my courage. I told him to get out and leave our house. He did, though he managed to accuse me of all kinds of things whilst packing his bag.

I was glad to see him go. I didn't care where he went or what he did. I needed him out of my life for good. All I felt was relief. I didn't cry. I rolled over and fell into a peaceful sleep.

Chapter Seventeen

The Smear Campaign

'A narcissistic smear campaign is executed by spreading lies and malicious content about the victim.

The narcissist does this by posting malicious comments on social media channels or other public forums. The goal is to harass and intimidate the victim, while also discrediting, defaming, and humiliating them.

Narcissists often use this tactic to get people who know the victim to turn against them and question their motives. This isolates their target and also reduces the chances of anyone believing them if they try to talk about the abuse they are enduring. The isolation and lack of support often result in the victim losing hope and staying in the relationship with the narcissist.

This is the abuser's end goal because it guarantees a source of continuous narcissistic supply.

How to Spot a Narcissistic Smear Campaign

Narcissists are very skilled in the art of propaganda and smear campaigns. They know how to manipulate others to do their dirty work for them and are masters of the art of abuse by proxy. In addition, they are experts at exploiting people's weaknesses, which is what makes them so dangerous.

The signs of a narcissist smear campaign can vary depending on the situation and perpetrator. However, one thing is certain: they are designed to damage your reputation or that of someone you care about. Some examples of signs include subtle remarks aimed at being hurtful, voicemails and emails with false statements, or even outright defamation on public channels such as social media.

How to Deal with a Narcissistic Smear Campaign

The best way to deal with a narcissistic smear campaign is to educate yourself about the tactics that narcissists use and how to counter them. One of the most important things to remember when dealing with this type of situation is that narcissists are not interested in what you have to say. They will also feel threatened by any criticism, and are prone to resort to displays of narcissistic rage.' (5)

I had prepared myself for the next stages of what may happen. I had done some reading on narcissism and behaviour and felt confident that I could predict the wave of emotions and actions that would follow. First, the hurting stage, pleading, admitting fault one minute but quickly switching the blame to me. I hoped I would be strong enough to do this, and not be weakened by his begging.

He started sending voice notes, instead of messages, something he used to mock other for. I knew his game. He wanted me to hear his voice, he knew it would penetrate deeper than a written word. I wasn't falling for it and stopped listening to them completely.

He accused me of hiding things. He believed he was entitled as my husband to ask me who I was texting if I was on my phone. He still accused me of hiding secret money. He accused me of planning to leave him for a long time and that I had just been playing the game. He claimed I had orchestrated the move back to the UK for this plan to unfold, ignoring the fact that it had been his idea in the first place. Over time these accusations would grow legs and become a fantasy world to soothe his ego and feed his image of the victim to whoever wanted to listen to him, mainly the *Flying Monkeys.*

A Flying Monkey is a popular psychology term that refers to an enabler of a highly narcissistic person or someone with narcissistic personality disorder. A flying monkey is an agent who acts on their behalf.

In everyday terms these are the ones who believe whatever the narcissist tells them, and in turn helps to do the dirty work by distributing the same rhetoric that the narcissist has been convincing themselves of, to ruin the victim's name and reputation.

They are the main helpers of *the smear campaign.*

He had a few. Luckily, I identified them quickly and was able to prevent what damage I could, certainly when it came to social media. They would message me, almost word for word accusations that he had thrown at me.

I was called a gold digger, a bad parent, accused of not letting him see my son, despite the fact he hadn't even asked to. It was almost laughable how elaborate some of the stories were. The ironic thing was that these people had very little to do with our lives, no clue as to what our life was like behind closed doors. Whoever really knows that?

I had to force myself not to be affected or upset by it, or to feel like I had to justify anything to these people. It was none of their business and they didn't know the truth, it was that simple. Nobody likes to think that there are things out there being said about them that aren't true, but by leaving a narcissist, you just have to hold it together and hold your head up high. It comes with the territory. Those who knew the truth were the only ones who count now.

He would post on Facebook a lot. Airing every piece of dirty laundry, he could, telling the world how evil I was. On one post he stated that he hoped I would die a lonely, painful death. He made an announcement one day that anyone he knew who was still friends with me would be removed as his friend immediately.

Who the hell did he think he was? As a result of this there are people that he has known for over 25 years that he now has nothing to do with, purely out of his petty belief that they have been disloyal to him, even though I have also been friends with these people for over 10 years. It was like being at school. In the end, I came off Facebook. Too many Flying Monkeys were providing him with details and photos of my life. It wasn't worth the hassle, and I no longer knew who I could trust. He would also keep creating new profiles, ones which I wouldn't know about and therefore block, like I had with his main one. It was tantamount to full-blown stalking.

Chapter Eighteen

Grey Rocking

'Grey rocking, or the grey rock method, is a tactic some people use when dealing with abusive or manipulative behaviour. It involves becoming as uninterested and unengaged as possible so that the other person loses interest. Some people anecdotally report that it reduces conflict and abuse.

The idea behind the technique is that abusive people, especially those with narcissistic tendencies, enjoy getting a reaction from their victims. Refusing to give them this reaction makes interactions less rewarding.' (6)

A friend had told me about this. The same one who told me to put my big girl pants on, incidentally. It sounded easy. It wasn't. Not giving emotive responses when someone is attacking you is extremely difficult. I would start off well, giving neutral responses. But he more I did, the more toxic he would become. Provoking me, goading me, desperate for my attention. I would eventually cave and before long we had pages and pages of messages back and forth. Bad start.

I got better though, and eventually he would get to a point where he would leave me alone. He knew I wasn't taking the bait anymore. It went from hourly messages, to only a few times in the day. Then from daily to weekly, until I got to the inevitable point of blocking him completely.

One minute I would receive a message declaring I was his whole life and he loved me - love bombing, I believe this is known as. The next, he would send vicious, disgusting messages that I was a lying, cheating whore. He even sent these messages to my dad's 75-year-old partner. He had no shame. He even accused me of having something to do with the burglary. He was losing his mind.

After the split he did everything I expected and more. I had known at some point I would have to cut him off completely. I couldn't even stomach the thought of speaking to him for a day more. At first, when I was using the grey rocking method, it was because I wanted to leave the lines of communication open, even if just to talk about or son, or any practical subjects to do with the house, or to discuss a divorce, but the anxiety I had every time he messaged me was unbearable.

As a result of cutting him off, he targeted my friends and family. He called my parents, my auntie, my friends, anyone who would listen to his carefully woven story which he had managed to convince himself was true. He was centre stage, and he needed his audience. He would relay back to me how sympathetic they were, claiming they gasped in shock at some of the things he told them. I didn't believe a word. Social media was clearly not fulfilling this adequately enough to feed his craving.

I lived in fear for the first few months that he would turn up at the door, drunk. He had never been physically violent with me, and I didn't expect that he would be, but the emotional threat was almost just as terrifying. He managed to get an email through to my work account one day to say he couldn't get a place to live and so he would have to move back in. If I refused, he would call the police as he was legally allowed access to the property by being named on the tenancy agreement.

The thought of this made me feel sick and scared. He said if I refused that he would turn up, get into the house and have the locks changed, banning me from my own house. Kind of contradicted his own point there, but hey. Every day would be a new message, a thinly veiled threat. 'Get ready' he said. Where his head was here in regard to our son, I have no idea. Thankfully, he got a house sorted and the threat was gone like a puff of smoke. I doubted whether he even had any intention of doing what he said. He loved to play mind games, he knew how scared I would be by even suggesting he came back, so here he was, still with some sort of hold over me.

I had changed the password on our security cameras, but I hadn't realised that he was the primary account holder and had access that I didn't. One day I was trying to figure it out on the app, when I noticed the amount of live streaming on the feed. I knew I hadn't been watching it live, and my stomach twisted as a realised what I had feared. He was watching me.

I scrolled through. There were countless times, day, and night. The middle of the night. I wanted to go outside and rip them all out. Somehow, I think he must have been able to see I had played them back. He messaged me and told me he needed to give me the passwords to get rid of his access. He told me it was tearing him apart watching us. What did he expect, for me to feel sorry for him? Those passwords were changed immediately, as well as everything else I could think of. Email accounts, train booking apps, everything.

He cut my phone off, but I didn't care, I was happy to change my number. I changed my car, I moved house. I needed to change as much as I could, be as anonymous as possible. I was scared to go out. He had moved back to our old town over an hour away, but I still didn't feel like I could walk down the street without fear of him appearing in front of me, I was terrified that

I would ever have to see his face again and look into his cold eyes.

Mixed with this fear was excitement that I didn't have to ask permission to do things that I wanted to. I felt like I had been released from prison. Our lives were instantly calmer, my son knew it and it made him feel at ease. I eventually met a friend for lunch, even though for the 20 minutes on the train I was looking over my shoulder, convinced he was watching me.

For the first three months he showed little interest in seeing our son, saying it was too difficult and upsetting. I knew for a fact that he didn't want to spend time with him, especially overnight, as in his eyes it would mean I would have too much freedom. I would be able to go out, to drink, to socialise. He couldn't bear the thought and he was still exercising a form of control by doing so. He wasn't thinking about what our son wanted or needed from his father. It was all about him and how HE felt.

Chapter Nineteen

Holiday madness

One thing I really wanted to know is what had happened with Irish Ian on that night out. I reached out to Ian and one of the other guys who I had also got on really well with, Darren. I didn't expect a reply and was surprised when Darren replied straight away. He was in a mess himself as his own marriage to his husband had also fallen apart. I asked him what had happened that night, and he didn't hesitate to tell me.

In a nutshell they had been in a pub called the *Rose and Crown*. Somehow, they ended up talking about Irish Catholics. He started telling Ian and Darren that he hated Catholics and when his dad was in the Army, he used to pour acid into the eyes of catholic children. Whether or not this is true I have no idea. Ian left the pub and went to Darren's bar, saying they would end up fighting.

Apparently, a bar stool had already been thrown. He then turned up at Darren's bar, still looking for trouble. He ordered a gin and tonic and hid it behind the bar. Darren was convinced he was ready to fight and use the glass to attack them. He promptly asked them to leave and closed the bar immediately. Now I knew. None of the story surprised me in the least and now I could understand why they cut him off. Ian eventually reached out to me and confirmed the story also. He told me he believed he was evil and never wanted to see him again. Fair enough, I thought.

In September, I took my son on holiday. He had begged me to go back to where we lived, he was missing his friends even more and I agreed, it might be a healing experience after all and there were friends who I really wanted to see too. I also needed more answers about the fallout with our friends. My son made sure his dad knew, the last thing I needed was being reported for kidnapping, after all. He didn't object, which I was mildly surprised about. I thought he would cause a fuss or create an objection.

We flew out early on the morning of the 27th, excited and looking forward to a week of escapism and friendly faces. As we came into land, I felt a mixture of emotions. Excitement, hope, but also sadness that for me, this country would always have many bad memories attached to it. We had organised a reunion at our old local for later in the afternoon, there were quite a few people coming, we couldn't wait. My son's face was lit up, he was chattering away like a monkey in the arrivals lounge, a sure-fire sign of his measure of happiness.

We stood at customs; the queue was massive. We approached the desk and handed over our passports. The female officer scanned mine. Frowned. Scanned it again. Silence. I waited for her to hand it back to me and send us on our way. She didn't. My heartbeat started to quicken. My son looked at me and asked 'mum, what's wrong?' I reassured him that everything was fine. Something told me it wasn't. The officer picked up the phone to make a call. My heart started pounding so fiercely I'm sure she could hear it. I looked around, the queue was gone, and we were the only ones there.

She finally broke the tense silence and said to me 'you need to come with us'. Oh god. My son's face was stricken, I felt sick. She wasn't speaking English to me now and I told her I didn't understand what she was saying. She was instantly irritated with me. 'But you used to live here, no?' I didn't have the full vocabulary to explain we had left a year ago and didn't remember half of the broken language I used to use. I asked her where we were going. 'The police station'. Oh god, oh god. I was racking my brains; had he reported me for taking our son out of the country? What else could it be? Was it a terrible misunderstanding?

We sat for what seemed like forever until they brought me a translator. All I could do was comfort my son and keep myself calm for his sake. The translator quizzed me. Had I taken something that didn't belong to me? I took this to mean two things, theft or kidnap. I asked if my son was anything to do with it, he said definitely not. Phew.

He left us for a while, the words rolling around and around my head. Something that didn't belong to me. I was baffled. I still had my phone with me so was frantically messaging people. The taxi driver – also a friend of my husband's – to tell him I didn't need him for a few hours at least, any friends who I could think of who may have a clue about why I was in so much trouble. One friend replied: 'What about your car, did you get that sorted?'

Fuck. The car, it was the car! It still sat in my friend's garage. For almost a year we had constantly called and emailed the lease company, and they still hadn't collected it. Then with the split, it had dropped down the list of priorities. Shit. I asked the translator if it could possibly be that, he said yes, it sounds like it might be. I relaxed. This was fixable. I had plenty of evidence to show my efforts for returning it. They didn't have a leg to stand on.

The main police officer dealing with me came to tell me I would need to get someone to come and collect my son. What? He said they couldn't release me until I had attended court, which was scheduled the next morning. I would have to spend the night in the city police cells.

I thought I might throw up. My son looked terrified. I protested; I told them there was no way they could separate us. They didn't care, they were just following orders they said. If I didn't have him collected, they would be forced to take him to a children's centre. 'Over my dead body,' I said. I doubt the phrase translated well.

I told them I would leave my passport with them and report back the next morning. No, that wasn't an option. Right. I frantically messaged everyone I trusted who could come and collect him. Most people were at work and couldn't reply. I had one option left. Irish Ian. He spoke the language fluently and knew the law. I also trusted him and knew that my son would feel safe with him.

He jumped in his car and came right away. He brought with him an air of calm and reassurance and told us it would be ok, it was clearly just an administrative issue which hadn't been communicated. My son visibly relaxed. I explained he would have to go with Ian for the night and he was fine with it, as long as I was ok. Fine! I'm fine! What's a night in cells in another country? I told myself it would be character building. There was no point getting myself into a state.

As soon as Ian and my son left the police station, they officially arrested me. They took my phone, my jewellery, I even had to take my laces out of my trainers. That was me now cut off from the outside world, and my boy. I felt numb really, I think that was better than being hysterical. I was amiable with the police, pleasant even. I felt like I needed them to think I didn't belong in this situation, I was a mother coming on holiday with her son, not a hardened criminal.

I had to sit and wait for the city police to collect me and take me to the main police station. At some point the main officer came to tell me that my husband had called. How? I wondered. I hadn't contacted him. I wondered if the police had told him that it was Ian who had custody of our son. That would go down well, not. Fuck it, I thought. How much worse could this scenario be?

The city police arrived. They looked at me, bored. The main officer walked in and spoke to me. 'You are lucky. I have managed to get you in court tonight. You can be with your son afterwards.' I felt like I had won the lottery. Anything now I could handle. My prayers were answered. Thanks, mum.

They took me in the police car to the main station as I still had to be fingerprinted. The car seats weren't actually seats, they were just one solid sheet of hard plastic. Bloody uncomfortable. Not quite the ride from the airport I expected.

They took me straight in, for the prints. The officer doing them couldn't have been more than 20. He was tall and spoke English. He reminded me of my husbands' eldest boy. His tone was friendly, and he asked me why I was there. He could tell I didn't belong. He made sure I had my bottle of water, as I was dangerously dehydrated from sheer anxiety. My spirits were a little higher, he even tried out a joke on me in his English. It didn't make sense, but we laughed anyway. He took my photograph. I kept getting an overwhelming urge to laugh out loud, this was ridiculous. I watched a lot of crime drama on TV and this felt like I was having an out of body experience, stood having my mugshot taken. Then, I was taken to the court, which meant I still had to be put in cells. This, I was not looking forward to.

The smell. Piss, mainly. It was cold, despite the 20 degrees or so outside. As I was led to my 'accommodation' I asked the officer how long I would have to wait. He shrugged; 'an hour, maybe two.' Ok I could handle that. I could work with timeframes. All I could do was sit and gather my thoughts. I was quiet, and the other cells were empty. Or so I thought. After a few minutes I heard a bloodcurdling scream coming from a closed cell which sounded close to mine. It was a man. He started smashing his cell door. A metal door, the sound was deafening. I put my hands over my ears to drown it out but there was no chance of that. He shouted, screamed, sang. Not just his mother tongue, but the odd bit of English too.

I have no idea how long I was actually there. It could have been 30 minutes, or 2 hours. I was stuck with this torture until my knight in shining armour dressed as a policeman came and called my name. It was time.

I was a lot more relaxed about the court experience, I had never been in court in my life but anything was better than being in that cell. I was given a translator and bundled into a courtroom full of lights and cameras. I was asked a few questions and it was over in minutes. Dismissed. Time to get my boy back. The relief was insurmountable, I was elated. I asked my legal representative where the nearest bar was and swiftly downed two large white wines while calling everyone I needed to. Ian brought my son to me and dropped us at the hotel, where we had a quick drink and collapsed into bed. Finally, the holiday could begin.

The next morning, he called my son's phone. He was hysterical. I had to take over the phone call as my son was getting upset. I breathed a huge breath before hearing his voice. He was screaming. He asked why I had been arrested and I told him. His only reply was 'good, you deserve it.' Nice.

He accused me of planning to stay there and never coming home. I'm not sure where he had got that idea, he knew we were coming for a week. He had been calling my dad over and over, even suggesting I may have tried to smuggle drugs into the country. What?

But his big issue, as predicted, was that we had called Ian for help. I had betrayed him, called on someone who he wasn't friends with anymore. How could I. Interestingly my son hadn't received any calls from his dad himself, and he also had Ian's number. Not once did he call that afternoon to check he was ok. Nothing said to Ian to appreciate that he had taken my son somewhere safe, until it was over. No no, all about him again, how his feelings were hurt because it was Ian who came to our rescue. It was pathetic.

He screamed obscenities to me down the phone. He told me he had visited a prostitute when we lived there together. Accused me of having an affair with Ian the whole time. He was disgusting. I didn't care anymore. I hung up and blocked any further calls. He left vile voice messages on my son's phone which I had to delete before he heard them, all punctuated with 'Say hi to Ian.' We had a lovely week after the initial stress. The car incident ended up costing me three thousand euros. I didn't ask him to contribute, I wouldn't give him the satisfaction.

Chapter Twenty

Is it me?

There is a wave of emotions involved in the process of leaving someone, especially when the other person makes you feel like you have done the evillest thing by ruining their life. You start to doubt your thoughts, your actions. Was I overreacting? Was I creating a monster out of my own perception? Was it me who was causing the problems?

Over time after many friends reached out to me, I know I wasn't going mad. They told me their true feelings about him. How they found it difficult to listen to the way he spoke to me. How they didn't understand why I never went out on social events, always finding excuses not to go. Some of them told me they had been forced to distance our friendship because they didn't want to be around him, they found him intimidating. I realised for years I had been too afraid of his reactions to stand up for myself and tell him I was going out and seeing my friends.

It had been a little different when we lived abroad, he always referred to us and our little bubble or little corner of the world. I used to think it was sweet and protective but in hindsight it was more like the bubble which meant nobody could get to us, to me. Just us really, with friends on the outside. Our close friends and family were all in the UK and I think he liked it that way. With my closest allies in another country, they were no threat to his happiness, and they couldn't tell me to my face that he was treating me badly.

Some of our best memories together were when we went away, either to a hotel or a holiday, just us. It was like he was a different person. I realise now that it meant that there was no risk to him from my loved ones who he believed would lure me away or convince me to leave him. Which he still believes is the case to this day. He still believes that I have lost my mind, that someone has convinced me to leave him. I've got it all wrong, we were happy, life was good. Nope.

This only became evident when we returned to the UK. Suddenly I was surrounded by those people who cared about me, and it made me extremely happy. As a result, his behaviour was noticeably worse, even around my dad who he loved, he became petulant and moody, and often ignorant.

We moved house twice in a short space of time and he refused to help with the moves. Friends and family rallied around doing the hard work while he watched rugby in the new living room. His friends would comment and call him names, but he didn't care, he would just laugh it off or tell them to fuck off. My 75-year-old dad would be up a ladder fixing a curtain pole and never would he offer to help. It was beneath him and he wanted to do what he wanted, as always. The truth was, he was pretty useless at DIY – it was a standing joke with us for many years. He hated this weakness, the inability to be the best at something. So he dismissed it and refused to try, to even show an offer of help. I think that was when my dad started seeing a different side to him.

Did he love me? Narcissists are generally incapable of real love. It was almost two years into the relationship when he told me he loved me, and it wasn't the most romantic of circumstances. He had kissed another girl at a Christmas party, hundreds of miles away from where I lay in bed. It made him 'realise' his feelings for me. I wasn't exactly overjoyed or swept away with romance.

Much later I found out that she had gone down on him publicly. Lovely.

Sometimes I did think he loved me. Despite the constant criticism, the put downs. He was still able to make me believe that he did. But in the last few years it seemed more like obsession and possession. Many people who are in controlling relationships believe they are loved but they are not, they are controlled, bullied, coerced. It is categorically not the same thing.

Chapter Twenty-one

Empathy

'Sometimes narcissists appear caring and empathetic. They may help a colleague at work. Be super romantic, especially in the early stages of a relationship. Or bend over backwards for their boss. And other times they can be cold and uncaring. Does this mean that narcissists have empathy, or not? Or do they have it sometimes? What's going on?!

Cognitive Empathy

Narcissists DO possess cognitive empathy. This is where they logically understand how you're probably feeling. They cognitively know when they insult you it causes upset. When they disappear for a few days, you worry.

A narcissists cognitive empathy helps regulate some of their behaviours. Because they know right from the wrong. And they know their actions affect others. The problem is they don't possess emotional empathy.

Emotional Empathy

Emotional empathy is where someone FEELS for others. It's not a conscious logical thought like cognitive empathy. It's instinctive.

For instance, you see a friend take a tumble. And you wince before they even hit the ground, anticipating their pain. Emotional empathy is rapid and automatic because it requires no conscious thought.

In another example, a friend may fail their driving test. You see how upset they are and feel upset too. Almost like it's happened to you. And you instantly know how to treat them because you feel it too.

Emotional empathy helps you understand others. And act in an appropriate and considerate ways. Because you FEEL what they're feeling. And these feelings have a powerful effect on your behaviour.

The Problem With Having No Emotional Empathy

Emotional empathy happens instantly, and effortlessly. It doesn't matter whether you're tired, stressed, or distracted. Your emotional empathy kicks in.

If you rely solely on cognitive empathy, then things can go wrong. You may be tired, have things on your mind, or be distracted in some way. Because your emotional empathy isn't there to automatically kick in, it's easy to neglect the other person's feelings.

For example, a narcissist may want a favour from you. But when they contact you, you tell them about something upsetting that happened earlier. Although they cognitively understand you're hurt, the narcissist doesn't feel your pain. And because they're so focussed on what they need, they forget your pain and insensitively ask for the favour.

Facade

As you're probably aware, narcissists operate most of the time under their "nice" facade. Especially when they're around people they want to impress.

The narcissist pretends to be kind, caring, and whatever qualities they think they need. This is to impress, and to fit in. And some narcissists are extremely talented at faking emotional empathy. They've spent a lifetime doing it. Narcissists can appear highly empathetic in some settings. And highly narcissistic in others.

For example, they may be the nicest person at work, if they want to impress their colleagues. But a complete tyrant at home. So, whilst they appear to switch between having empathy and narcissism, this isn't the case. They NEVER have emotional empathy. They fake emotional empathy when they're on their best behaviour, and when they want to impress. And when they want to let their hair down, the narcissistic behaviours come out.

Faking Emotional Empathy

Narcissists spend their lives faking who they are to fit in. Ultimately, they want to be loved and adored. And that means being on the right side of some people.

Many narcissists become experts at faking emotional empathy. They use their cognitive empathy to understand what emotion they should be feeling. Then their acting skills to fake that emotion. If you watch a narcissist closely, you may see the moment they "decide" to feel something. There's often a pause. Cognitive empathy takes time. Because a decision needs to be made about what feeling to project out. Whereas emotional empathy is instant, because it's instinctive.

Narcissists make mistakes faking emotional empathy, especially in unusual situations. For instance, someone's cat may have died. And the narcissist has never met this situation before. They don't know how they're supposed to "feel". So, they insensitively laugh, thinking that's the best response.

Agendas

Narcissists may also fake empathy to further their agendas. At work they may want somebody's job. So they patiently wait.

They wait for that person to slip up. Make a mistake, or do something they shouldn't. Then pounce all over it.

The narcissist wages a war on that person for their actions. And passionately explains to anyone who listens why it was so wrong. People may notice the narcissists over-the-top response. But admire their passion for "doing the right thing". Not realising they're using it for ammunition for selfish motives.

These narcissists are often wrongly attributed with having high levels of emotional empathy. Because they always seem to have a moral fight on their hands. But the truth is they just want a fight. And use the pretence of emotional empathy to justify it.

Acquisition Of Empathy

Narcissists often target highly empathetic people for roles as partner and friend. And one obvious reason for this is because these people are easier for narcissists to manipulate. But there's also another reason.

Narcissists are empty shells of people. They don't connect with their emotions, and don't really know who they are. To hide this, they find empathetic people to copy. Narcissists take mannerisms and phrases that display emotional empathy and use them as their own. Making their empathetic act even more convincing.

We Often Assume They Have Empathy

It's natural to assume that others think similar to ourselves. And it's easy to attribute some of the narcissist's behaviours to emotional empathy.

For instance, a narcissist husband may take his wife to his bosses' dinner party. Where he treats his wife kindly and compassionately. Making sure she feels at ease in a room full of strangers. It's easy for her to joyously conclude that he cares. But this isn't the case.

Really, he wanted to impress his boss. And show him what a wonderful caring and compassionate person he is. He knows his boss likes that type of thing. So whilst he appears to be behaving empathetically, it was actually for his own benefit.

In another example, someone may insult the narcissists partner. And the narcissist leaps to their defence, in what appears like an act of emotional empathy. What a hero! They must care right?! Really, the narcissist took the insult as an insult to themselves. "How dare you insult MY Partner". And reacted in self-defence, rather than in empathy for their partners feelings. Just like if someone insults your car. You're not angry because you feel for your car. You're angry because it's an indirect insult to you.

In many situations we wrongly assume the narcissist has emotional empathy. Because their actions are sometimes the same. But hidden underneath, their motives are different.

Narcissistic People

Some people have high levels of narcissism, but not enough to be diagnosed with narcissistic personality disorder. These people display flashes of both narcissism and empathy, depending on the circumstances.

If a narcissistic person becomes involved in a conflict, they may display high levels of narcissism during the row. And respond in an over-the-top and cold way. But later calm down and see the err of their ways when their empathy kicks back in. And offer a genuine apology for their behaviour.

These people may behave like narcissists when triggered by stressful situations. Then return to empathetic behaviours when all's well.

Some people who are thought of as narcissists may actually be narcissistic. And not have the full disorder. Which explains why they switch between empathy and narcissism. Narcissistic people do have emotional empathy. But not in all situations.

If someone switches between narcissistic and emotionally empathetic behaviours, then it's either a narcissist faking empathy, or someone who's narcissistic, switching between the two. Alternatively, it could be us, wrongly assuming their behaviours show empathy.

Narcissists have cognitive empathy, but no emotional empathy. So they use cognitive empathy to fake emotional empathy. And some are so skilled, they fool close family members for years. Particularly when they take character traits from empathetic people they're close to. People fooled by their facade see a nice empathetic person suddenly change into a narcissistic person. Like Jekyll and Hyde. And wonder what happened. They don't realise this is the narcissists true self. And their mask has slipped.

Just remember, a genuine narcissist doesn't have emotional empathy. All their actions are self-serving. Even when they're apparently being empathetic and kind. When a narcissist shows emotional empathy, it's always worth questioning their motives. (7)

If I ever had a bad day, he was not interested. He was completely immersed in his own world and problems at all times. In the end I wouldn't bother sharing my problems with him and then he would turn it around on me, saying I wasn't telling him the truth, or I was hiding things from him. I couldn't win either way.

He was scornful about everything. If my friends were going through anything he would laugh about it, almost as if they deserved everything they got. More so if they were my best friends. It was like he wanted me to agree with him and eventually turn on them. The more I fought their corner, the more he would shoot me down. My loyalty to my friends always stood firm and he found this difficult, it was one barrier he could not, and did not break down.

One night I fell over on a dark road, while walking home, seriously spraining my ankle. I was crying with agony and all he did was laugh and told me to 'man up' It was his two children who actually helped me get up and look after me. If it was the other way around and he was injured or ill however, he would expect round the clock care and attention from me, and I would often give it.

Chapter Twenty-two

Nature or nurture

I often wondered in generally if people who displayed narcissistic tendencies were simply born with them or if it was a product of their past or upbringing. It seems it is a widely discussed topic:

'Like most personality disorders, narcissism is something of an enigma. You might think the narcissist is just someone who is very selfish, but there is a distinct difference between narcissism and selfishness. Are we genetically hard-wired in some cases for self-centred and self-aggrandising behaviour? Or are we influenced by our environment and our upbringing? Can past trauma create present narcissistic behaviour? Or as might seem logical, is narcissism a combination of all of the above?

There are varying opinions as to what triggers narcissistic behaviour, as well as to how broad the spectrum of narcissistic behaviour might be. Many experts agree that narcissism is caused by a combination of factors, from genetic predispositions to environmental circumstances to childhood traumas. Depending on the case, one factor might have more weight than others.

If you've ever wondered what causes the formation of narcissism, then take a look at the following factors.

Is Biology Destiny? How Genetics Might Play a Role

In some relatively recent rethinking of narcissistic personality disorder, as with psychological disorders in general, many scientists are now suggesting that there may be some genetic roots to the cause of narcissism.

It is known that individuals with narcissistic personality disorder have less volume of brain tissue in the left anterior insula. This is the region of the brain responsible for empathy and emotional management. This suggests that a narcissist's very genetic make-up might be at least partially responsible for their lack of compassion, inability to feel guilt, and dysfunctional cognition. It also indicates that the potential link between narcissism and sociopathic behaviour grows out of genetic deficiencies. It might be that some narcissists truly cannot help but act the way that they do.

In addition, other researchers have argued that narcissism is linked to physical attributes. This describes a concept known as "reactive inheritance," which suggests that someone's actual appearance shapes their personality and behaviour. These studies note that most people who exhibit pathological narcissistic behaviour are physically attractive and/or athletically talented.

Nature and Neurobiology: Linking Thinking and Doing

There are also clear links between brain development and the circumstances of childhood. That is, if a child is abused, neglected, malnourished, or otherwise mistreated in significant ways, this prevents the brain from developing fully and normally. While this isn't innately genetic, it certainly points to a biological explanation of narcissistic behaviour.

This argument suggests that narcissism arises from the interplay between genetic predisposition and environmental influences. If someone is born with a smaller anterior insula and is raised by a loving and caring family, then they may or may not develop narcissistic tendencies. But if they are raised in a dysfunctional atmosphere, then the chances are much higher that they will begin to display narcissistic behaviours from a young age.

There is also the suggestion that narcissism may provide some evolutionary advantages. Because narcissists are skilled at coercion, they potentially have advantages in mating, at least in the short term.

Additionally, narcissists are dominant within any given social group, so they are better able to access and take advantage of whatever resources (food, water, shelter) the community possesses.

Family Bonds and Childhood Harm

The environment in which a child is raised, including the ways in which the parents interact with the child, clearly plays a significant part in the onset of narcissism. When interpersonal relationships are dysfunctional or abusive, children can develop coping mechanisms - whether those methods are psychologically helpful or harmful - in order to defend themselves.

If either or both of the parents display narcissistic behaviour, then a child is much more likely, regardless of genetic considerations, to exhibit the same traits. If a child is exposed to harsh criticism for even the slightest of infractions or lavished with excessive praise for even the smallest achievement, then these learned behaviours will become a part of their own family dynamic later in life. There is also some evidence that overindulging a child can cause narcissism.

Even if parents aren't narcissists, per se, a child who suffers from neglect or verbal and physical abuse can develop narcissistic personality disorder as a way to cover their lack of self-esteem and confidence. Parents whose emotions and actions are unpredictable can also cause a child to hide behind the self-aggrandising characteristics and psychological manipulations that are hallmarks of narcissism.

Certainly, parents are not the only influencing figures in a child's life. A child who is surrounded by extended family and indulgent friends may present with narcissistic behaviour later in life. If a child is constantly praised or admired without needing to do anything much, then they might develop an outsized ego and a sense that they can do no wrong.

Triggers and Transformations in Adults

Most diagnoses of narcissistic personality disorder don't occur until someone has reached adulthood, 18 or older. This is because, in the first place, people are still forming their identity and personality throughout their youth and teen years (and, of course, often beyond that). It is also because many children exhibit narcissistic behaviour, which is quite natural as your superego (compassion for others) develops after your ego is formed.

So, narcissism that may present itself in young children or even teenagers may simply be a part of the process of becoming a full-fledged adult. These characteristics may dissipate over time as the child becomes more socialised, as the teenager becomes more thoughtful in their actions. If these tendencies don't fade away, then you may be dealing with someone who technically has a disorder. In many cases, narcissistic behaviour is triggered by events or circumstances, so that narcissistic personality disorder may be latent until significant life changes reveal it. For example, a serious relationship or marriage can trigger the behaviour, or the birth of a child.

Narcissism can also develop over time, as previously suggested, and someone with genetic predispositions or environmentally relevant factors may slowly slide into narcissistic behaviour. For example, someone with tendencies secures a powerful position at work which triggers a growing narcissistic response full of entitlement and exaggerated successes.

While narcissism can be the result of a difficult nurturing environment, there is also evidence to suggest that it might also claim some genetic and biological causes. Most likely, narcissism develops out of a complex set of interactions between genetics, biological development, childhood circumstances, and situational triggers. It's not nature *versus* nurture; rather, it's nature *in tandem* with nurture. (8)

His childhood wasn't the best, in his eyes. His father left home when he was 11 years old and moved to Wales, and from what I am led to believe, he had little contact with him in his formative years. He married again.

His relationship with his mother was difficult; he was constantly in trouble, getting in with the wrong crowd, fighting and rebelling against everything. He used to tell me elaborate stories about how his mother treated him, how she tried to get rid of him, how she used to beat him. Many years I later was given a very different picture from the woman herself. He grew up bitter, full of hate. They had little money, his mother bringing up two children alone. He used to wear hand me downs from other kids and was teased and bullied at school. He resented his father for abandoning him and his mother for not being able to give him the best of everything. His behaviour spiralled out of control, and he moved in with his nanna, before joining the Army. It was either that or end up in prison sooner or later.

His childhood I believe created a serious inferiority complex within him, regardless how much of it was hard fact, or how much was in his own fantasy world.

It very much related to a narcissistic personality type. Always wanting the best even if he couldn't afford it. Always trying to prove his worth, his status as a man. He spent beyond his means and then sulked when he was broke as a result. He would constantly refer back to not being able to afford things when he was a child. If I ever talked about my childhood or the things I had, or did, he would bring it straight back to him every time, already playing the victim at every opportunity.

He would make me feel like I had a privileged upbringing and resented it. I didn't, my childhood was normal, uneventful, safe. We weren't rich by any stretch. My dad worked full time and my mum was a housewife for most of her life. It had its challenges when I was younger, my dad worked shifts, and I felt like I never saw him. I didn't understand why he wasn't there every day for me. We had the inevitable years of rebellion when I hit my teens where I would feel anger or frustrated with him, but as I got older, I understood the sacrifices he made. I respected him, trusted him, and loved him unconditionally. I had always hoped that one day I would meet a man just like him, who stood firm on his loyalty and principles.

I only met his father a couple of times. He was intense, full on, just like his son. He told me he fancied me. I found that odd and mildly disturbing. I wrote it off to banter. He died suddenly of a heart attack in 2013 when our son was only 2 months old. Ironically, he was immediately put on a pedestal; promoted to 'best father' status, posthumously. He was great, charismatic, charming, the best. My son even has his middle name after him. Forgotten were the feelings of abandonment which plagued him for years, instead these feelings were recycled, redirected; to me.

I also wondered if I had been responsible for some of his behaviour. I cooked, cleaned, did everything in the house, and he let me. I could have tried harder maybe, pushed back and asked him to help more. In the later years I did just that, but the damage had already been done. Maybe I had mothered him so much that these were now his expectations and was I being unreasonable to then complain about it?

The truth is, I did all those things as it was easier to do them myself. If he cooked, he would smash up the kitchen in a blind rage if he couldn't find something or if the ingredients weren't stored in his way. If he cleaned, he would throw things, put our belongings in the bin if there was anything on the floor. On more than one occasion I would be looking through the bin's days later, looking for my son's toys. Like I said, it was easier to take matters into my own hands.

After three months apart, he eventually agreed to have our son to stay with him for a few days. It was a complete disaster. My boy called after two days saying he wanted to come home. He was upset because his dad had been bad mouthing me to him and others and my son obviously found it very upsetting to listen to.

He would show my son paperwork from the bank, or text messages. He would tell him I had left him with nothing, despite the two vans full of his belongings and the furniture we had mutually agreed to splitting (after several vicious emails). Anything to show how awful mum was. All completely out of context of course and extremely confusing for a young boy. Thankfully he knew what his dad could be like and was very protective of me. He didn't go back there for a while.

A couple of months later we arranged for him to go every other weekend. On one of those weekends, he accessed my son's phone and managed to get into my Facebook and Messenger account. He screenshotted over 20 private conversations I had with friends and family and sent them to his phone, therefore leaving them on my sons' phone to see. I felt sick. Even now he was violating my privacy. Looking for dirt, for ammunition against me. I didn't think he was capable of stooping so low but clearly, I was wrong. He was desperate and it achieved nothing.

There are still things that remain on his terms, which is frustrating. The fortnightly visits from his son are dependent on me driving the 86-mile round trip. He won't come to our town to pick him up. He claims it is 'too traumatic.' He has me over a barrel – I either take him, or he doesn't get to see his dad. On this I put my sons interests before anyone's, and I do it. It galls me, but it's a battle I'm not ready to start yet.

One night when my son was staying with him, he had clearly gone out and left his older son to babysit. It was getting late and my son text his dad asking where he was. His reply was 'Balls deep in a fat bird, living the dream'. He was a disgrace.

He still tells my son regularly that we split up because I was sleeping with other men. That I was hiding money and leading a double life. He tells him I'm having an affair with my boss at work. I was forced to have an awkward conversation with my boss about it, to give him a heads up. We all worked in the same industry, and it was likely their paths would cross. He didn't care how destructive his comments are, to others, even to a child. My son is now 9 years old.

Interestingly not long after he left, he received a bank statement for a savings account I didn't even know existed. I had opened his mail, always had done since he didn't. Yet again projection came into play here, accusing me of what he was doing himself. He had borrowed money from me the week or so before, claiming his wages were gone. Funny that he didn't mention the 6k that I could see sat in this account, and I could also see he was transferring money into it from his personal account. Convenient maybe so that when he showed me his balance, it would always be low. Clever.

Another letter I opened as I could see it was from the police - and to be honest I didn't check the name, I assumed I had been caught speeding. It was for him. Caught doing 99mph in a 70 zone. Oopsie. I sent a photo of the letter to his son and told him I would make sure he got it.

A couple of weeks later, another letter. He had sent a half-hearted attempt at a declaration back to the police, not even signing it. I sent another message to his son, who quickly received a message from his dad, to 'tell mummy it's an offence to open someone else's mail but I won't report the offence this time.' I wish I had just binned it. He told me to return it to sender, so I did. After I moved from that house, I rarely got passed my old mail and really there shouldn't had been much. Anything from him was returned to sender, as per his wishes.

Some months later my son sent me a text while he was at his dads one night. It simply said, 'You're going to court.' That was nice. Turned out dad had received a court date for an impending driving ban, and I was now being blamed for not forwarding his mail. He left 7 months ago and suddenly it was my fault for not taking his mail? I don't think so. I just laughed. It was no longer problem. HE was no longer my problem.

Its 7 months to the day as I write this. Life is becoming calmer, but I still feel the rattle of unpredictability in the air. I still worry about ever having to see him. I still get anxiety when my son is with him, knowing I will be mentioned. I know over time this will get easier, but it still bothers me that this excuse of a man will still be tied to me no matter what.

People ask me if I regret anything. Did I regret meeting him, have I wasted 10 years of my life? No. Those 10 years have shaped me as a person, redefined my strength and made me re-evaluate my needs and wants from a relationship. We have a wonderful child together so I can't regret that. He on the other hand feels differently. He says he wished he never met me; I have wasted those 10 years of his life and he can't get them back. One day, I hope he sees things differently but I'm not holding my breath.

Chapter Twenty-three

Out with old, in with the new

There are a few reasons why the narcissist flaunts the new supply. First, it is a way to invalidate the old supply. Second, it is a way to show off how much better they are than the old supply. Third, it is a way to make the old supply feel jealous and envious. Finally, it is a way to show the new supply how much power and control the narcissist has. (10)

Narcissists quickly move on to others, as generally they struggle to be alone. They crave the attention too much from others and it doesn't take long for them to pull people in, using the charm and persona they have perfected so well.

It was a matter of weeks before I was being told of other women in his life. I didn't care. In fact, that for me just meant that his attention would be elsewhere and not on me for once. I was told by friends that he was up to no good when we lived abroad, which correlated with his confession about the prostitute. It wouldn't have surprised me in the slightest and just further confirmed where his jealousy originated from. It no longer bothered me; I just pitied him.

I often wonder if his ex-wife saw me as the new supply. Maybe she was relieved that he met me, so that she could move on with her life. I have never met her, never spoken to her, maybe I never will. I'm sure we would have plenty to talk about.

I also pity the women who may fall under his spell and live to regret it. Would I warn them? That's a tough question, I don't know. If I did, I would only have one thing to say:

To those women – GET OUT.

Chapter Twenty-four

The future

I filed for divorce less than two months after we broke up. I would have happily done it the day after but knew I should probably let the dust settle. I was naïve to think that would only take a few months, but I needed to do it sooner rather than later. As I predicted, he ignored it, missed the deadline. He would email me to tell me that he wouldn't challenge the divorce, as he couldn't wait to get rid of me. Fine by me, I thought. But as per usual action speak louder than words and he still wasn't responding. He was controlling the situation, yet again. Making me wait. He even sent me a screenshot of an email he had sent to the court:

'I wish to see the grounds for divorce as I suspect I will wholly disagree, that woman, she kept me in a false life, maintained a

sexual relationship and its my belief she was having extra marital affairs and I have seen messages to corroborate these thoughts. She has lied and left me with debts undisclosed, she has hidden money and has undeclared earnings and assets not shared with me. This will not be a straightforward divorce I shall be seeking financial audits and some interventions that will show what a lying manipulative individual she is and ensure that financially she pays her way as she has lived a charmed life thanks to my 10 years of hard graft. I have 2 bags of clothes, coffee table and sideboard to show for my hard work.'

I actually laughed out loud when I read this. Never had I heard so many lies or narcissistic comments in such a short text in my life. A charmed life? 2 bags of clothes? Hidden money? So called evidence of affairs? Maintained a sexual relationship? Wow. This man actually *believed* his own lies, that was evident. If that's what he was telling an admin assistant in the court, then I couldn't imagine what he was telling his friends.

If I ever get angry at these words, I am able to pull myself out of it quickly due to one simple fact. I know the truth. My conscience is clear and those who know and love me, know that. That is all that matters. I am true to myself now more than I ever have been and *that* is my future.

Epilogue

Being controlled is a powerful thing and you may feel like you can never be free. You may feel like you are not strong enough. When children are involved, it brings with a whole load of additional complications but for me, that was my motive. I couldn't let my son grow up in a toxic environment any longer. He was already intimidated by his father, and it would only get worse. I also couldn't risk how it would affect his behaviour when he was older. I talked earlier about nature vs nurture for a very good reason. My son could have grown up thinking that was an acceptable way to treat women. I would have never forgiven myself. I hope that the damage is not already done, but it is my job to create his environment of support for his future. As a mother that is my duty.

I owe so much to my friends and family, many of which I spoke to on a daily basis. They gave me the strength to keep going and would remind me of why I was doing this, should I ever voice any doubt.

I hope if you are going through anything like what I have experienced, that you can find the strength to be true to yourself too. You are not alone, don't ever think of yourself as a burden to others, and there is a way out, you just need to find the inner fight within yourself.

References

1. Narcissistic personality disorder - Symptoms and causes - Mayo Clinic
2. These Types Of People Magically Attract Narcissists (innertoxicrelief.com)
3. 9 Traits of a Misogynist: Is Your Partner One? - Kim Saeed
4. How Narcissists Use Gaslighting (choosingtherapy.com)
5. Narcissistic Smear Campaign - how to spot it and what to do about it (carlacorelli.com)
6. Grey rock method: What it is and how to use it effectively (medicalnewstoday.com)
7. What Is Stonewalling? (verywellmind.com)

Printed in Great Britain
by Amazon

18687183R00108